BEYOND SUICIDE

BY RYAN F. MCKNIGHT

TABLE OF CONTENTS

FOREWORD

Rev. Lynnessa H. Joyner-Robinson, CEO & Founder

GIFT'M (Grace is for the Messy), LLC

Several years ago, I had the privilege of meeting a young man who struck me as compassionate, caring, and bright. He communicated well and liked to joke around. At first meet, he appeared like a regular young guy, but by the weekend's end, I picked up something. A distinct sadness that hung around and seemed to show up in his eyes the more we shared and communicated to one another our history.

You see, I was marrying into Ryan's family and although I am genuinely deeply interested in people's lives, I had a vested curiosity as he would be a part of my family and I his. It was a crisp October fall, Saturday afternoon when we met. He was warm and relaxed from the start, but as our weekend unfolded, I noticed and began to discover there was more to Ryan than met the eye. It became clear to me that when we talked about our upbringings, a sadness seemed to peek into his eyes, and they would get dimmer. I had questions!

As we've come to know each other, over the course of time, I learned more and more about Ryan and my questions began to be answered. I realized he needed to get things out. He needed a safe space to pour his heart out. I was honored to be a part of that space and over the years, we've had many in depth conversations. As you read his story you will discover his genuine experiences are

1

authentic. You will be struck by how much he cares and encouraged by how much he understands!

As you read this book, you will experience the same symbolism I experienced. He draws you in! You see, to me, his asking me to be involved in this book symbolized that I was a safe person and he trusted me. We'd created a bond, and you too will feel his heart and passion for caring and healing! You will see his particular concern for young people who may be going through many of the same things he's writing about.

Ryan will talk about hopelessness, loneliness, suicide, and suicidal ideations due to unhealed trauma that may or may not have unwittingly been inflicted upon you as children. He delves into adults, acting like children, caregivers, who don't care and doctors who don't listen.

There is an additional caveat in this book that is crucial to Ryan's message. He's a man and according to the National Institute of Mental Health (NIMH), "the suicide rate for men in the United States was 22.8 per 100,000 in 2021, which is four times higher than the rate for women, which was 5.7 per 100,000. This means that men have a suicide rate that is over 3.5 times higher than women." The data speaks for itself! Men are at particular risk due to the very things Ryan will reveal to you as you go along with him on this journey!

We all know it is incredibly difficult to talk about pain and even more excruciating for men because of the stigma and complexities around mental health for them. Well, imagine how much harder it is for young men! Yet, Ryan has found the wherewithal to write it all down, collect his thoughts, put them in some form of order and then chronicle them so it makes sense to us as we read this book! This is no small feat and yet somehow, Ryan has accomplished this goal! That is who Ryan is and it is remarkable!

This book is going to help that young kid who is hiding behind their pain because as they take the courage to read, page after page, they will know they are not alone! Ryan has been where they are and if he made it out, they can too!

Read on young warriors and fight for your life! You are loved, you are healed, and your life is worth it!

Ryan and I understand!

PROLOGUE

The first thing I noticed when I arrived upon the shores of peace in Delaware was how quiet it was. I grew up in a neighborhood that was right next to a major road. On the opposite side of the neighborhood was a slew of railroad tracks, one of the most active railroads in the country. Overhead we had commercial airliners flying out from the airport every few minutes, so I always thought of our town as the doormat of the sky. Finally, we had all manner of motorcycles, and music pumping cars ripping down our street at night. When I sat in our backyard to relax, there was nothing but noise, not to mention the activity of our neighbors living around us in close proximity.

All this activity made my eventual permanent exile and subsequent arrival to a new place of peace like the most profound slice of heaven. No noise, no screaming cars, and planes. No clacking trains, no crazy neighbors. Just quiet. It may seem like nothing to some of you, but you don't know how powerful it is to grow up in a place of hell and be delivered to a place where there is none of that, only peace.

You, my readers, are about to embark on a journey with me. My journey, my life, my hell, my peace. I went through it all for a reason. I went through fire and death so that I may impart the wisdom of what I learned for your benefit. I have cleaved my heart open and laid the contents bare so that you may be healed, so that your lives will be saved, so that you don't have to go through what I went through. Don't waste or squander the gifts of my heart.

They're what I have now. They made me what I am. So, learn from them. Learn what it means to be taken all the way to the edge of death. Learn what it means to return to life. Learn what it means to move beyond suicide.

PART 1 - HELL: THE ABANDONMENT

CHILD'S LIFE

As children, we are often unaware that we are depressed, because we don't understand it. This is usually where the depression begins in our lives. We fool ourselves into believing it started much later, but really, it started in our childhood. Our parents unknowingly teach us to wear a mask and hide our true selves.

It's easy to be unaware of things when we are children. It's not until you are older that you begin to realize that your problems are directly attributed to something that happened in your childhood.

In my case, it was my parents' divorce. It hurt me far more than I realized. It also hurt just how much I was kept in the dark by everyone in my family, my siblings included. No one told me squat about squat, and then wondered why I was so messed up.

And it was one of my siblings who told me about our parents' divorce, not my own parents. Unbelievable, right? My sibling said, "Mommy and Daddy aren't going to be living together anymore." After reading this, my siblings are probably going to tell me that they didn't think I could handle being told about the divorce.

Yet I had a close friend who lived across the street, and his parents were divorced. So, I was familiar with what it was like, and how unpleasant it could be. I experienced the poison between my friend's parents. They were nasty bad to each other, and that didn't change for as long as I knew them.

So, before they make that excuse, this should go to show my siblings that I was not clueless as a child and would have been able to stomach the truth. This was an abandonment by my parents, who should have sat the four of us down and told us exactly what was happening, together. A sit down may have happened with my older three siblings, but again I don't know because no one told me anything.

When we are children, our parents offload their behavior into us. We copy them. This happens at a subconscious level as well as a surface level.

Our parents' behavior becomes deeply ingrained in us. This has a tremendous effect in how we develop, and who we grow into. Our very identities are shaped by our parents, until you come of age to make your own choices.

You may start to see the poison left inside you by your parents. Parts of them that are not really who you are. So, if you are wise, you will cut these pieces out like cancer.

You do this so that you don't become a mirror image of those who procreated you. Otherwise, you spend the rest of your life fighting the same battles and the same demons that they did.

MOTHER

It's difficult for the perpetrator to understand their part in abandonment. My parents could not relate to me on any level. So, the abandonment started when I was a child. I felt so empty; it seemed I was in this world all by myself yet living in a house full of people.

The relationship between my Mom and I was very sharp and perturbed. Emotions between her and I were highly charged. The relationship was different than it was between her and my siblings for one simple reason. In the conflicts between my Mom and siblings, there came a point where my siblings would roll over and let her win to stop her nagging. They gave in.

I did not. I knew that she was wrong, and I was right. I knew that she had obtuse characteristics and I never stopped letting her know it. This resulted in more fights of greater intensity, and it did not stop. She just kept coming at me. This went on for years upon years, my entire childhood and adolescence. She did not stop and kept fighting me up until the very last few days I lived with her. Those days were particularly fiery and personal. I don't mean this as a personal insult toward her, but it seemed as though failure as a mother completed itself in the end.

It was as though it came full circle with me, her last and youngest child out of the nest. The most destructive, explosive, and brightest fireworks finale of failure. It was bursting and blasting through the night sky, heard by God and the heavens themselves.

This was all because she didn't know how to handle me. It's difficult for a mother to teach a boy how to be a man. Often, my Mom used to tell me that I was just like my Dad. It's not wise to compare a child to his or her parents. The reason she compared me to him was because I didn't roll over like my other siblings. I stood my ground and fought. I fought her with an intensity comparable to my Dad. That's why she felt that way.

I can give you a prime example of how behavior can be passed down from parents to children, often with children not even realizing it, and at that point, they have become like their parents.

Once, at a young age, my Mom had an experience with her mother. My Grandmother told my Mom, "I don't understand you. You don't love me anymore."

Jump forward to the relationship between my Mom and I. One day, when my Mom was particularly livid with me about my choice not to start college after high school, she said to me, "I don't understand you. You don't love me anymore." I felt like I was living in a time warp, and nothing around me was real.

FATHER

The thing that made me so angry with my Dad was that he was clueless as to my anger. Sons should be able to look to their fathers for guidance, security, love, and life preparation. It's sad that I could not get that from my Dad because he never got it from his father.

In an effort to help me understand Dad, my Cousin pointed out that my Dad thinks I hate him. I did not hate him, the person. I hated the things he did and didn't do.

Now that's the thing that would make me angrier with him. How he didn't know why I was angry. But really, deep down in his heart, I think he knew. As I have learned what it really means to face your fears, I clearly see that my Dad just hides things deep down, and turns away from it all. Runs away even. Because the truth is too horrifying for him to handle. The world in which he lives is unreal because he chooses to remain there and thus it has become his truth. Part of my anger and frustration has subsided because I have learned his truth is not my truth.

I couldn't stand to be in his presence, to look in his eyes, or even have a conversation, because he did not acknowledge my suffering. It's like it didn't exist to him.

Now that's raw pain. It's rage inducing when your closest loved ones, who are supposed to understand you, have no idea what you're going through. Even worse, they don't agree with the source of your suffering, because in order to admit the truth of it, they have to admit that there is something wrong with them. They will not do it.

As forestated, neither my Great-Grandfather nor my Grandfather had the right relationships with their sons. As a result, my Uncles, my Dad's brothers, have accepted this dysfunctional relationship as being reality.

Unfortunately, this characteristic has been passed down from Dad to his children, my siblings, who in their own ways have made up their own kinds of reality.

PARENTAL PAIN

I've forestated the nature of who my parents are and my time with them, or lack thereof, but I've yet to cover some of the finer points of the fabric of their being.

They both caused me great pain, agony, and suffering on a colossal scale. Pain can exist in many forms. However, pain begotten by family is the worst. It's one thing when you are injured by a friend, acquaintance, or stranger. It's another thing entirely when you're wounded by your own flesh and blood; not just once, but over and over and repeatedly for years and decades. That's enough to make you want to kill a person.

Let me make this abundantly clear, the same way this book is going to show you death, it's also going to show you life, as well as hate and love. For as the song writer wrote, "There is a Balm in Gilead, to heal the sin sick soul."

This is the kind of agony I received from my parents. I begin with my father, whom I didn't really get to know until later in life. As a child, I loved him very deeply, as I did with all my immediate family.

However, he was not around long. My Mom drove him up and out of our house due to her idiocy and deplorable interpersonal relationship skills. My Mom was a nag. And so, my Dad didn't know how to deal with her nagging ways. So, in the end, he opted to abandon us all to get away from her, and his emotional responsibilities as a father. For in truth, the man was not equipped with the knowledge and experience, from parental guidance, to be a competent and loving father. His frustrations went beyond my Mom; it was also his ignorance in dealing with us kids. It was not knowing how to raise children, and the failings that resulted as such. In his anger, he would take that out on us.

He became a good provider, paying child support, but once again, because of my Mom's financial shortsightedness, my siblings and I barely saw any of that aid enriching our personal lives. Instead, she used it to pay for things she deemed important.

I do not fault my Dad for his abandonment of me and my siblings. I know that if he had not, then something truly terrible would have happened between him and my Mom.

Although, when a son is abandoned by his father, or he simply has no father from birth, it leaves a hole in his heart which is in the shape of his father. It's not a healthy thing being a young boy without a father figure in his life. He has no means by which to be forged into the man he needs to be. Again, only a father can teach a boy how to be a man, not a mother. A mother can teach her son life values and home ec, but she cannot teach him the transitional stages of manhood. Why? She's not a man.

And so, it was with my Mom and me. I had many immaturities in my dealings with my Mom simply because I had no father to teach me what was right, like how to honor my father and mother. I did things that were wrong. I wronged my Mom. But at the time I didn't know that many of these things were wrong, or in other cases, I simply didn't want to know. Because back then, in my eyes, she was all the way wrong, and I was all the way right.

Now, in many ways, this was correct, but not all ways. My Mom was horrifyingly wrong in most capacities with how she dealt with us, her children. She was right about some things, of course, like our need and duty toward household chores which would help her out; many a time we simply did not respect or honor these obligations.

The results of these traits lead to catastrophic damage in her children because we were not prepared for the dangers of the world. And so, the world tore us apart because we didn't know how to deal with it.

An example of this is when I experienced bullying from a classmate who was trying to get me to date another female classmate in the sixth grade. Now, make no mistake, the kid brought punishment on himself for what he was doing. It was harassment because he did it every morning without fail for several days. But when I told my Mom the extent of what was happening, she went to the school and lied about what was really going on.

In truth, the kid was openly and publicly attempting to make me face this dating situation, which was very stupid. This was a form of bullying.

Now, my Mom lied on this kid and said that he was threatening me and stalking me on the way home from school, because I walked home every day.

Tell me something, my readers, how the heck did she go from harassment in the form of dating a female classmate, to threatening and stalking me? How did her mind translate this into that delusional output? How warped could her mind have been to arrive at that terrible conclusion which caused me years of turmoil at school?

Mind you, my readers, immediately after this happened, I saw the fruits of this harmful labor that very day at school. I remember we had a school assembly in the auditorium. I heard the kid call my name from behind me. I turned to see him sitting several rows back with his friends, some of which were close friends of mine.

The kid held up his detention papers and said, "Hey Ryan! Thanks!" He looked very pissed with me. Accusatory questions were thrown my way, some of which were from my close friends. The outcome completely blindsided me. I was totally confused as to what had happened, and was receiving fierce judgment, hostility, and malcontent towards my personal being.

I didn't know what exactly my Mom told the teachers, staff, and principal because that was done in private between them. I thought after that I could rest easy, and it would all go away. I was wrong.

I tried helplessly to explain things to my friends how I didn't know what had happened. Clearly, they still didn't approve. Nor did many other students. Understand, my readers, this was a popular kid, and my Mom had just reported him for being a bully. That, in their eyes, was me being a rat fink. You just didn't do that, which in its own essence is completely brainless, stupid, and boneheaded because basically what that means is they view their social lives as being more important than their mental, emotional, physical, and spiritual wellbeing.

I experienced this as a great betrayal on my Mom's part. I simply couldn't believe she'd done this. She took a dire situation and made it exponentially worse and drove me into depression. From that point on school became hell. That kid did not stop causing me trouble for two years, using the few opportunities he had to taunt me. Thank God I was protected. I know that if it wasn't for God, I would never have made it through that. God kept me separate from this kid for most of my middle school years. We had no classes together, we were rarely in the same room, but when we were, I was downright panicking. When I saw him in the halls I panicked.

We made peace later. I don't know what God did, but somehow, He resolved the situation, and Moved that kid's heart. Because he became more like a good friend. I know that my friends were defending me from him behind the scenes when he spoke badly of me, and I suspect that they may have been responsible for getting him to let it go. I believe the kid's mother also played a part in bringing him to peace. But ultimately God is the One who put that fire out so that I wouldn't die from it. Again, thank God it didn't come to a physical fight between us because I believe he was certainly capable of that if we both lost our heads and emotions started flaring.

That is the extent of the trauma that my Mom put me through at school. The one thing about her that I could not stand in this situation was that my outrage did not move her. She genuinely believed that she was not wrong. She was convinced that she did right and had no part in how the matter declined into madness. She would often tell me in the most obnoxiously childish voice, "I'm not wrong!"

The fact that she took this stance and infantile attitude only poured fuel on the fire of pissivity that burned inside me, and for years drove me to keep throwing this incident back in her face repeatedly. She had ruined my life at school. I hated her for what she had done. How could I not? She would never concede to the fact that she had made a mistake, an oversight, undersight, or any other sight.

Failure was a foreign word in her mind; she believed she was incapable of such a thing. This belief was born out of the situation she grew up in.

My Mom was born into a household of dysfunctional people. As a result, she and her siblings suffered from this dilemma. My grandparents, her parents, lacked good parenting skills, and so their children grew into the most self-absorbed, ill-mannered, attention-starved people. This was a breeding ground for insecurities. And those insecurities, in part, developed into an indominable iron will that they could do no wrong, and that they were gods. I have never before in my life seen a group of people that were more egomaniacal, haughty, stubborn, and insufferable. Living with one was more than enough. Seeing them all together on a family vacation was a godless spectacle, no pun intended.

Case and point, I'm sure my own Mom was quite confounded by the fact that I would never give in to her will and wishes, especially after the bullying incident at school. After that sequence of events, I saw her true nature. I saw what was really inside her. And it was something that, even as a child, God was not going to allow me to give up in subjugation to this dysfunctionality.

Things continually got worse as the years passed. My relationship with her deteriorated. When I say my Mom was a nag, I mean that even the sound of her voice was naggish. It made you want to get up and smack her. Things started getting downright dangerous in the atmosphere of the house we lived in. The constant warfare between us was not just emotional, but spiritual. The spiritual warfare became so intense and unending, that the house we lived in became a stomping ground for bad spirits.

What people in our society don't understand is this world is more than physical, it's spiritual as well. And every choice you make carries spiritual significance and consequence. If you are a positive person and think positively, then your home atmosphere will be positive; there will be peace and prosperity on a spiritual level, which God will work through to bless every aspect of your living. If you are a negative person, then your home atmosphere will be negative; there will be toxicity and destruction on a spiritual level, which the devil will use to seep into every aspect of your life.

Yes, this was the crazy crap that I had to deal with and grow up in. And I thank God that I made it out of all that; that I made it away from my Mom. Because I can promise you this, my dear readers, my Mom was seriously hurting me little by little, every single day of my life with her nagging, negative, uncompromising, ironclad stubbornness, and prideful atmosphere. She was driving me toward suicide. She was driving me towards the rabbit hole that I would never come out of.

And if I had not left Ohio, left her far behind, I was going to kill her. Let me say that again and be explicit. I was going to take my Mom's life. I wanted to; it was premeditated because she would have driven me to do it in some fit of psychotic rage. I know now that eventually I would have reached my limit and snapped. I can tell you that it was getting close to that point. My relationship had become so toxic with her that I would literally stay in my room, away from her, to escape those intense battles.

Later, I understood perfectly that this was what my Mom put my Dad through. If Dad hadn't left, he would have killed her, or she would have killed him. Either way, somebody was going to die.

My Cousin knew that something was very wrong in Ohio. He could feel that the relationship between myself and Mom was swiftly heading into violence. One day, my Cousin and Dad were riding in the car together, and my Cousin informed my Dad of the situation.

Life in Ohio had reached the minutes before cataclysmic explosion. He told my Dad, "If we don't get Ryan out of Ohio, we will either be visiting him in jail or in the cemetery; or we will be visiting your ex-wife in jail or the cemetery. If you don't act on this, their blood will be on your hands, and you will have to explain to God why you let that happen. I know it's going to be hard us having a young man living in our little apartment, yet because he's your son, and my cousin, it needs to be so."

Five minutes of silence passed between them before Dad finally agreed that they should come get me. That's my Dad for you. He's a Negative Nelly of the first order. Always overthinking and too much fear. That is what truly caused me pain, anger, and rage toward him. The simple fact that his mind wasn't first concerned with my well-being. There was always some wayward negative thought that he would allow to stop him from seeing what was truly important. My life and survival.

His mind was lost in places of, "Oh, I don't know how we're going to have the money for Ryan to stay with us." Or "Where is he going to sleep?" "We're working all the time; we'll barely see him."

His OCD was kicking in, big time. There was a simple fear of having his son living with him, strange as that sounds. But beyond that, the man simply did not deal with his own personal problems before I arrived. Problems that went back decades into the past. Places where he was still broken, even before he met my Mom.

And he was given instruction by my Cousin, as well as Cousins who live across the planet, that he needed to make some pivotal and crucial changes so as to make things easier for me to settle into my new home in Delaware.

The problem was he did not make these changes. Not even a little. He did not change his character before I arrived, and I had no idea, at the time, the state of my Dad's mind, spirit, and emotions. None. Zero. I was happily walking away from one broken parent, and not realizing that I was walking toward another broken parent.

Once I realized the severity of the person I was living with, I became filled with rage. I couldn't believe this was all happening again. That I had traded one dysfunctional parent for another. That threw me for a long time. I could not abide that. I had no intention of tolerating this madness a second time. The inconsiderate nature of a man who was not thinking how his actions affected others, especially myself. I was so angry by the fact that this man had refused to change his ways for me, so that I would not have a repeat experience on the apocalyptic scale of living in Ohio.

Sadly, and unfortunately, however, he failed here. So, I, along with my Cousin, had to endure Dad's insufferable atmosphere for years on end. And my Cousin had to endure it even longer than I did, since my Dad moved in with him years before I arrived.

I only survived Dad because of my Cousin. My Cousin's unconditionally loving nature. His steadfastness in the face of adversity, insanity, all things negative, and his calming presence, made all the difference I needed. Without him, there is no doubt in my mind whatsoever that either I would have killed Dad, or he would have killed me. Just like with Mom.

Just to give you an idea of the situation throughout the years, if you took my Cousin out of the equation, there would be no relationship between my Dad and I. "It has nothing to do with you." My Cousin told me. "It's him." The reason for this is simply the nature of who Dad was. He didn't know how to be a dad.

He feared uncomfortable silences between us, so he would talk your ear off until he gave you a headache. He constantly needed approval to fill the hole in his past, which was that his father never gave him attention or approval. As a result, when the three of us were watching movies together, he would never stop talking. His questions would always end in, "Right?" You don't know how many times I heard that word, "Right? Right? Right?"

He had this abominable habit of needing to know everything; needing to understand everything, and it was insatiable. And he never seemed to run out of energy in the pursuit of useless and worthless knowledge. Again, we would be watching movies, and my Cousin and I couldn't enjoy them because Mr. Need To Know over here has to stop and ask questions not just every scene, but every line the characters speak.

He was looking for answers to questions that neither of us had. It got so bad at one point, I told him, "Why don't you write the director and find out?" My Cousin said later that he had to do his best not to laugh. I didn't care, I was frustrated, annoyed, and pissed. After that, my Dad was quiet.

I have a memory of when the three of us were about to watch a movie that Dad brought home from the library. I asked, "What's the movie about?" He went off into a long spiel about who the actors were in the film, who the director was, the producer, the writer, and the awards that the film won. I looked at him and said, "That's not what I asked you. What's the movie about?"

That actually threw him for a spin, because he does not receive information in the manner it's presented to him. He receives it against the backdrop of his experiences. This causes his responses to be tapered by what he feels answers the question.

Another example, on our way home from Breckenridge, Colorado, my Dad had an accident and was hospitalized for two days. When my Cousin and I went to pick him up, the discharge nurse asked my Cousin a question, which he responded to. My Dad got incensed and stated, "I can talk for myself, and don't need you to answer for me!" So, as you can see, Dad did not process the nurse was talking to my Cousin, not him.

What I didn't understand at that time was that he took these instances personal. He has the habit of taking everything as a personal insult; that people are making direct attacks on his person whenever they speak truth to him. He can't take it. He can't take directness. He can't take forwardness. He can't stand us making the major decisions on matters.

Let me give you some more examples. I have never before in my life witnessed a person with the level of obsessive-compulsive disorder that my Dad has. He is a creature of habit to the core. He will always lay the TV, DVD, and stereo remotes side by side in the same position, always.

My Cousin tested this. My Dad put the three remotes side by side, pushed together in a neat row, then went to fetch some food from the kitchen. My Cousin took the remotes and laid them about haphazardly. Dad came back in, saw the remotes, and put them back together, side by side, neatly, and perfectly just the way he had them previously. The man's mind isn't right until such mundane things are corrected.

My Cousin was in the hospital once, and when he got well and came home, he still had the hospital bracelet on his wrist. My Dad offered to cut it off with his pocketknife. My Cousin refused. Dad offered again several more times throughout the day. My Cousin continued to refuse. Dad's attention was fixed on the wristband to the exclusion of other thoughts. Indeed, of all things, a hospital wristband was what occupied his attention, and was driving him mad. My Cousin knew it was making him crazy, and that was his intention. It was these little pleasures we were able to get out of the situations that would make us laugh and keep us human.

My Dad never had to wash dishes in his childhood. His mother did all that. So, as a grown elderly man, it would never occur to him to have to wash dishes. It was ingrained in the neural pathways of his brain. And when he did occasionally wash dishes, he didn't clean them adequately. So, if my Cousin and I wanted to have clean dishes, it was essential that we wash them.

Now, because of my Dad's No Dish Washing Policy, I ended up doing more of the dishes than anyone, due to my Cousin's health issues. What flabbergasted me was the fact that Dad would fill that wash basin up with dishes in the blink of an eye. In one day, that thing would be full. He never washed anything right after he used it. He would leave every last utensil, bowl, cup, dish, and whatever in that sink for someone else to wash. And to him that was no problem.

Not only that, but he would never reuse dishes. He will eat off one plate and use a fork, throw them in the sink, then five minutes later, he will grab a bowl and a fork, eat out of that, and then throw them in the sink.

One time, my Cousin and I went up to Boston to visit with his sister. It was a wonderful familial visit, and an all-around good couple of weeks. My Dad stayed in Delaware, however, and when we arrived home, he was happy to see us, even though his pride wouldn't allow him to admit that. When we got home, I was fuming pissed because I discovered that the basin in the sink was filled to overflowing with all manner of dishes. Literally overflowing. I was so pissed that I didn't even try to hide it, "You've got to be kidding me!" That's what I yelled when I saw them. And I know Dad heard me. My Cousin heard me too and inquired, so I told him.

My Dad had gone two full weeks without doing any dishes at all and waited for us to come home to wash them. And the man didn't see anything wrong with this. That is the depth and level that his habits and inconsideration run to. Man, I was so mad that I couldn't be around him. I went in the bathroom and stayed there awhile. My Cousin had a conversation with Dad out in the living room, telling him how wrong that was, because my Dad genuinely didn't know why I was so angry. Seriously, how clueless can you be?

His eating habits were disgusting too. He would use a butter knife to eat out of a peanut butter jar, lick the knife, and put the knife back in the jar to continue his peanut buttery feasting. Needless to say, my Cousin and I never touched those jars from then on. We wouldn't touch a lot of things that he touched, period, because he didn't wash his hands enough.

Another habit he had was that he was always watching us like a hawk. When we watched movies especially, he was glancing over at us repeatedly. He did it quickly too, thinking he was hiding it from us, but we could clearly see him doing it. My Cousin explained to me that Dad was watching our reactions to things, reactions to movie scenes, because he didn't know how to react to them himself. A person who doesn't know who he/she is will watch others to see their behavior toward life. They then mimic this behavior.

One time, my Cousin counted the number of times that Dad looked over at him. Thirty-two times in the span of a half hour. I eventually developed a kind of wall on the table which sat in front of me. I used partially filled plastic water bottles to create a barrier for me to hide behind due to my Dad's constant hawkish peeping. Anytime we had guests over and they asked me about my water wall, I would joke and tell them, "It keeps the demons out." This was truer than they realized.

The honest truth is this. If we did not do things a certain way with my Dad, then we would have conflict eternal with him. He's that sensitive.

The last memory I have to say about Dad is quite simple, but very revealing. My Cousin had to go to the hospital one night. He was going through Atrial Fibrillation which was only exacerbating his Congestive Heart Failure.

In other words, his heart was beating irregularly, and wouldn't stabilize, which was causing his breathing to go out of control, and since his heart was already in bad condition, that meant that he was at death's door.

My Dad and I took him to the emergency room, and they put him on a ventilator. A bad experience to be on one of those machines because it basically forces your breathing into a certain rhythm, pushing your heart and lungs to come under control. Whether you could keep up with it or not is a bit of a question.

I was next to his bed the whole time, scared out of my mind. I believe now that I was in shock. Shock because I could feel in my own body what was happening to him. I felt the spirit of death in my flesh and soul. I could feel my own heart beating in strange ways. I could feel his bodily trauma and there was nothing I could do. That's how closely linked God has me to my Cousin. Our spiritual bond is strong enough that I can feel when his body is suffering as if it's my own, as well as what he's facing spiritually.

There have been few times in my life when I've been that afraid, and let me tell you, I was afraid. This was the first person and parental figure I had ever met in my life who not only understood me and all I had been through but stood in my corner of life against all threats or forces that would try to harm me. He was and is a powerful man of God and his body was trying to die. The devil was really trying to take him out. And I told him, as I held his hand, that if he doesn't make it, then I'm not going to make it. I told him that flat out and meant it fully. I said it because it was true and because I hoped it would give him the drive he needed to stay on this plain of life.

Again, God gave me a close bond with this man, and he was at death's door, so that made it feel as though I was dying with him. I mean that literally, it felt like my body wanted to shut down too. I've not felt anything like that since the experience happened.

Thank the Lord Almighty, who is a Healer and Deliverer, that after several hellish hours of being on that ventilator his breathing stabilized and he came through. But it was only because of God, not the machine. The machine wasn't getting the job done. That was very clear.

God interceded, and so we both lived. I escaped death yet again and so did he.

Now, where was my Dad in all this? Sitting in the corner of the hospital room behind me, staring at his phone. The whole time. He never said a word to his Cousin. Yes, that is right. His own fears and insecurities of being in an uncomfortable environment meant that's where his head was at. Not once did he come to our Cousin's side and offer any kind of comfort. Dad didn't take his hand, like I did, to offer solace and the simple human knowledge and presence that he wasn't alone as he fought to survive.

No, my Dad, who has known my Cousin for over forty years, and is a spiritual brother to him, sat in the corner and played on his smartphone.

The man was dying. If there was ever a time to be close to him, it was then. To this day, I don't know all of what was going through his mind, but I do know that there was fear. Fear not of the deathly situation, but fear of the world around him.

Dad has a very annoying habit of being nosy. He'll eavesdrop on our conversations from the next room. Sometimes my Cousin and I would be talking in his bedroom, and my Dad would stand near the doorway to the room, inspecting the DVD collection on the wall. He pretended to be interested in the DVD's so that he could stand close enough to hear our conversation.

So, I explained that to say this, my dear readers; this is the clincher. My Cousin told me later that at the very moment in the hospital when I told him that I wouldn't be able to live on without him, my Dad actually leaned over closer to us, whilst pretending to be busy with his phone, in order to nose in to the conversation and listen to my words. That's where his head was when his Cousin was dying right in front of him. Dad knew what was happening because the doctor explained that, if in forty-five minutes, his condition does not change, they will put him in an induced coma, and intubate.

That's what I mean when I say that my Dad lived on a whole other plain of mental and spiritual existence. In the face of death, my Dad's mental habits would still reign supreme.

I will never forget that until my dying day. I've forgiven it, but how can I forget something like that? It made me truly wonder about him. That'd be like if you were busy throwing a party at your house while at the same time, you can see through your window that a family member is hanging off a cliff outside.

And my last example is this. We were getting ready to go on vacation. My Cousin and I packed the car and got it ready for our departure. When Dad came home, he opened the trunk, saw the way we packed it, took everything out, and repacked the car to his liking. I don't think I need to say anything about that for you to see, readers.

I believe I've given you a pretty clear picture of who my Dad is, and what I had to contend with whilst around him. Now, readers, you can see that I walked away from one parent, who made me want to kill myself, and into the presence of another parent who had the potential to make me want to kill myself, but for God's protection in the form of my Cousin who was the only reason that I was kept steady and level.

He protected me from my Mom, pulling me out of Ohio and away from that deadly life; for it was my Cousin's will, not my Dad's, to get me out of that hellhole.

My Cousin told me later, that before I arrived in Delaware, God told him that I needed to be protected. And that's exactly what he did, and I will forever be grateful that God put one person on this earth, created with the charge and purpose of understanding me, and protecting me from all harm. Because I had a destiny to fulfill. That destiny is in the form of this book, which is meant to bring to suicidal people the message that I understand what they've been through, and to spread God's protection over them. This is what the devil was trying to kill. The devil was trying to kill me because killing me meant killing my destiny; it meant killing this book to stop it from reaching out and saving people's lives.

This book is equally to demonstrate that relationships can be healed, i.e. father, mother, siblings, and other family members.

God and the devil are real, y'all. And people have forgotten all about this, willfully. Which is why this country is in the sorry state it's in. We've moved away from God. It's time to move back.

SIBLINGS

First off, it must be known that there is a considerable age gap between myself and my siblings. I am the youngest of my parents' children. This inevitably placed some distance between us in and of itself.

I was in elementary school by the time my eldest sister was going off to college. I was beginning middle school when my second eldest sister went off to college. I hadn't even finished middle school by the time my brother went off to college.

I was so overjoyed when they came home for breaks because I didn't even have a relationship with them to begin with before they left.

I loved them all so very much and still do. I loved them unconditionally from my earliest recollection. Even through the chaotic, insane, and confusing atmosphere of our household, I loved them unconditionally. I had nothing but love for them. Pure love that could outlast all the negativity surrounding me. I just wanted them to love me back. That's all I wanted from them. I didn't know at the time just how much I craved their love.

They loved me, but I did not feel nor understand their love.

The overarching reality of sibling love is foundationally taught and observed through parental love. Thus, dysfunctional families can only display dysfunctional love, which is not love at all.

FRIENDS

The poor relationship with my siblings further enhanced the abandonment of my friends. I did not know how to love them as brothers due to the lack of love in my own family and our household. Realizing all this made my life a miserable hell.

Friendships during the middle school years are supposed to be enjoyable, memorable and long lasting. Mine caused a tornado effect and I was caught in the vortex. I had to live through the whirlwind of taunts, strange looks, emotional and phantom bullying.

As a result of four elementary schools worth of graduates merging, I was now faced with people I had not known from kindergarten to fifth grade. Fortunately, I learned from my Cousin that some friends are seasonal, while others are meant to be in your life until the day you die. Those are called lifelong friends.

Now, I had to be about the business of separating seasonal and lifelong friends. When it comes to my friends and classmates, my acceptance of the concept of friendship brought about difficulty; because it appeared all my friends fell into the seasonal category. Conflict was generated in my home because my Mom tried to force these seasonal friends upon me, while I was trying to break away.

On one occasion, my Mom suggested to my friends to come over to my house, unannounced and while I was alone. I was upstairs in my room. No knock at the door because my Mom told them where the key was for the back door. At the time, I'm hearing the back door opening, not knowing who it was, nobody announcing their presence, and I could hear footsteps on the kitchen floor. For all I knew, someone had broken into my house.

To my parental readers, this kind of careless activity will cause extreme panic attacks in your children. I overheated, had red blotches on my skin, sporadic breathing, heart palpitations, a severe pain in the chest as though someone punched or hit me with a hammer.

I was thrust into a world of paranoia, so much so that my nerves caused me to not want to live; it also caused guilt in me as though I did something to lose those friends. But I was not guilty.

I could not make my Mom understand that these were seasonal friends and our season of friendship had ended. But she tried to basically cram them down my throat. I am fully aware that she was not nor is a mean-spirited person; rather, she thought she was doing something good. Parents, please learn how to listen to your children.

SILENT SUFFERING - ANTIDEPRESSANTS

'Silent Suffering' could be used as a metaphor to describe the condition of many high school students; their general state of being in everything that they go through in high school. Although, in this case, I'll be using it more specifically to describe a certain kind of suffering.

I'm talking about 'Antidepressants'. You know what I'm talking about, kids. Those lovely medications that your parents got your bodies hooked on. The ones that slowly kill you. I'll go through my experiences with these medications to show anyone who doesn't know what they're like. I hope it helps those of you who did go through this by showing you that I identify with you.

Here we go. It's been over a decade since I first started being on those meds. I believe I was fifteen years old when I started using medication. Back in this time, I was pretty well into my depression. I had been for a long time. Much of it feels like a blur now. I'll try to recount as much of it as I can.

I remember feeling helpless; helpless in the doctor's offices and clinics, with my Mom sitting nearby. The psychiatrists prescribed the meds, and I was on my way to an early grave.

Even before taking the meds, I felt hollow. On the meds, I felt numb, and what do you know, the meds were the cause of this numbness. They made me feel like a zombie. I was so doped up on this stuff. My dose had to be high because I was walking through every one of my days at school without any care about anything. I felt nothing. When kids insulted me at school, or were rude, or anything unpleasant or traumatizing happened, I didn't feel it as much.

I felt absolutely exhausted all the time, I couldn't stay awake in class. My teachers saw this, and treated me with a mild amount of disdain, which at the time made me feel they were cold, heartless, and aides in facilitating my suicide. When you're suffering on the inside, it makes everyone seem more cruel.

When I got home, I would sleep until my Mom arrived from work. I had no energy to do my homework immediately, nor was I in the emotional or mental state to do it.

Usually, I'd get a half night's sleep or less every night. I slept terribly, even with the melatonin I took. In all, these meds did not help in the slightest. If anything, they were just helping to dig my grave.

That's not the way the psychiatrists explain it though, and definitely not the way my Clinical Counselor explained it. They say it's meant to balance you.

Apparently, kids, the professionals have diagnosed you with depression. That you have low levels of a chemical in your brain known as serotonin. Their answer to your problem is to raise these levels of serotonin by pumping you full of drugs that are chalk full of serotonin.

"Serotonin, also known as 5-hydroxytryptamine (5-HT), is a monoamine neurotransmitter. It also acts as a hormone. As a neurotransmitter, serotonin carries

messages between nerve cells in your brain (your central nervous system) and throughout your body (your peripheral nervous system)." **clevelandclinic.org**

They've got our well-being down to a science, y'all. As if science has never failed us before, has never been wrong before, and is the answer to everything. That's a load of malarkey if I've ever heard one.

So why don't I feel balanced? Why do I still feel depressed? Hmmmm. News flash, everyone. Antidepressants are not meant to fix you; they're not meant to make you happy. They don't solve any of your personal problems.

Please do yourselves a favor, and ACTUALLY LISTEN TO SOMEONE WHO HAS BEEN ON THESE MEDS, AND DON'T LISTEN TO SOME IGNORANT PROFESSIONALS WHO HAVE NOT BEEN ON THE MEDS, WHO ACT LIKE THEY UNDERSTAND. THEY DON'T.

This, my readers, is the purpose of this work. I believe God allowed me to live so that I could be a witness to others. To help you, my good people. I have suffered, and I know you have too, greatly. I am not here to repeat what all the other self-help books say. My experiences are raw and real. I am here for you, to speak to you, to speak to your spirits and emotions and minds.

I do care, unlike some of your clueless health care professionals. Many of them are at their jobs for a paycheck, and the more people they can prescribe the meds to, the more money they can make. It's all about money, people, they don't care about you. They don't care about your health, your past, your life. They care about drugging you, anyway they can, to make a quick buck. You are nothing but dollar signs to them. Accept it.

Now let me get to the whole point of this chapter. All across the landscape of our so called 'great country', we have kids who are going through terrible things. Personal problems at home with their families, bad neighborhoods they live in, poverty, abuse. The world has problems, for sure.

Particularly at home, parents don't know how to raise their children anymore. They don't know how to protect, or they do know and just choose not to. Or they believe they're doing nothing wrong, and are just killing their children faster, unbeknownst to them.

So, the kids already have problems right off the bat, at home. They live in chaotic environments. And you are a product of your environment. You live in a racist household, then most likely you will grow up to be a racist. You grow up in an abusive household, then most likely you will grow up to be abusive, fearful or both.

Then these kids have to go off to the brutal torture known as high school, where unbeknownst to many parents, is a place where kids are just surviving day to day. It's a place that parents have forgotten about because they have forgotten what it was like for them to be kids. That's because with each generation the dynamics change. Schools have changed, and so has the generation of kids. It's different.

We're taught a load of malarkey for twelve years, learning very few precious skills we will need when we become 'productive members of society'. That, and to a great degree, some teachers in our schools don't really care about the students, and again, are just there for a paycheck.

When I was in school, I never felt the sense that it was a community. I never felt the sense that my teachers cared about me. In fact, I got the very real sense that my teachers were very uncaring for me, save for a few. And even they were not exactly what I'd call mentors, close teachers.

This is what kids have to deal with when they're growing up in those very turbulent years of hormones. They're growing up, so they don't know who they are. They often have a very rough start to life, based on their home conditions. School is hell. So, they begin to break down.

They often have suicide attempts now; they have for a long time. It's gotten much, much worse in the last two decades. Then, based on suicide, or the way that their kids are behaving, and because the parents don't know how to help, they start to think there is something wrong with their child. So, they see their health care professionals and get their children drugged up on antidepressants.

The sad part is the parent or parents at the foundational level are at fault. How can it be something wrong with your child? You are the one responsible for them. For their growth, their well-being. If something is wrong with your child, if they're not going in the right direction, then I promise you it's something you did, allowed, or didn't do for them.

Again, how can this be the child's doing when outside factors generated the depression and anxiety? THEY'RE CHILDREN. They don't know anything.

They're just starting their lives. It's your job, PARENTS, to teach them how to be men and women. To teach them the skills they need to survive in this society.

PARENTS need to accept the fact that they played a part in their child's suffering, whether they like it or not. The children didn't get this way on their own. That's a fact whether you want to accept it or not.

Shame on you for putting your kids on medications that radically effect their bodies and their minds.

Let me rephrase this and say it very slowly for those who are slow.

Antidepressants... are... not... the... same... as... the... acetaminophen... pills... in... your... cabinet...

They... are... not... vitamins...

They... are... not... cough... drops...

They... are... SERIOUSLY... STRONG... psychotropic... medications... meant... to... alter... your... brain... chemistry...

They... also... have... TERRIBLE... SIDE... EFFECTS... AND... WITHDRAWAL... EFFECTS...

Effects... that... will... MESS... YOUR... BODY... UP...

AND I MEAN THAT IN EVERY SENSE OF THE WORDS I AM SPEAKING TO YOU NOW. THESE MEDS WILL SCREW YOU UP. YOUR PSYCHIATRISTS, CLINICAL COUNSELORS, NURSE PRACTITIONERS, AND PHYSICIAN'S ASSISTANTS, WILL NOT TELL YOU THESE THINGS. THEY DO

NOT TELL YOU THE PRICE YOUR BODY WILL PAY
FOR BEING ON THEM.

Because they want you on these meds for the rest
of your life. Do you not see this, or understand this? They
put you on the meds for good… They don't mean for you
to get off your meds… It hurts me to say it, but it's true.
Please, believe me. I know. These drugs are designed to
keep the patients on them for the rest of their lives.

When my Clinical Counselor got me in touch with
professionals who would start this drug process, I had no
idea what I was getting into. I had various people prescribe
me meds over the years, but eventually settled on a
psychiatrist who I primarily went to see for a few years.
The psychiatrist was nice. It wasn't until years later, when
I had grown, did I realize that my psychiatrist was just like
any other.

I'd go in, talk to the psychiatrist alone, and tell her
the same old crap. Inside me, nothing felt different.
Sometimes I think that maybe we need to drug up some of
our doctors, clear their heads, and let them get a good look
at their own results. Maybe, they'll have an epiphany. Or
maybe they'll be just as clueless and indifferent as always,
just like the pharmaceutical overlords they serve. The ones
who line their pockets so that the suffering can continue.

High school itself is suffering, nowadays. Children
suffer through it, they hate it. I'm sure this is not true
everywhere in the country, but to a very large extent it is.
What's more is that many of them, and I do mean many,
are on antidepressants. It's a way for them to attempt to
deal with their problems.

But most, if not every child keeps the fact that they're on the meds a secret. They don't dare talk about it. They don't even tell their best friends. Why would they? Why would we? That's just the way. You're not supposed to talk about those kinds of problems. Society trains us to think that admitting our own personal problems is a weakness. Let me repeat. THE STIGMA OF SOCIETY PREVENTS OUR CHILDREN FROM DISCUSSING THIS.

We don't ever want anyone to know that we are on antidepressants. It's humiliating, right? It tells everyone that you're depressed. You're unhappy. So, we internalize it and act like everything is alright. We act okay around our friends at school. You put on a fake smile and mingle to survive. You don't mingle to make friends; you mingle to keep them around so that you can survive the day. You're basically using them as your human shields.

I never told anyone in school that I was on these meds. Now I understand that a number of my classmates were probably on them too and just kept it secret like me. I call this 'Silent Suffering'.

How amazing is this. An entire generation of children who are so ashamed that they cannot even admit to one another what they're going through. What does that say about us? We're lost children. You're lost. Plain and simple.

It's our parents who didn't do the job right. Your psychiatrist convinces you that there is something wrong with you. That there is something wrong in your brain. You start to believe there is something wrong with you because everyone close to you is saying so.

The crazy part of all this is that they actually convince you that you need it, like it will help. They enter into this soft place of middle ground with you. And in that place of feeling a little better, maybe a little bit of hope, you say, "Yes. Maybe that will work." Then they've got you on their hook, sucking the life out of your body. Now you're just another dead person walking, another corpse just waiting to happen. You might as well just say that you're dead, because you sure aren't alive when you're on those meds. This is how you kill children, families. Maybe, you can all learn how to treat your children better by reading this.

Children, there's nothing wrong with you. You just didn't have the right people around you, guiding you from the beginning. The male parent who teaches you how to grow from a boy into a man. The female parent who teaches you how to grow from a girl into a woman.

There are good parents out there and there are bad parents out there. Sadly, a large number of them don't do a good job, so children act out, and do all kinds of insane things nowadays.

Personally, I believe with all my heart that antidepressants only help to kill you faster. They just deaden you more than you already are. They make your lifeless heart turn to dust, which then blows away in the wind.

This is not a joke, people. They don't help you. They make it worse. They make everything worse. They kill you faster. Psychiatrists and the pharmaceutical companies are just a bunch of unindicted genocidal monsters, and only a step above the common street pharmacist aka drug pushers. They're killing us, killing you.

Is that really so hard to believe?

SIDE EFFECTS MAY INCLUDE...

You've heard all those wonderful things they say on commercials about medications, particularly antidepressants. They say things like, side effects may include "thoughts of suicide." "If you feel these symptoms, consult your doctor immediately."

Most recently, I observed four commercials. The first was an asthma drug that possibly causes parasitic infections. The second was a different asthma drug, competing with the former, that also causes possible parasitic infections. The third was an arthritis drug that can cause thoughts of suicide. The fourth was a psoriasis drug that can cause cancer and reduces your immune system.

Yeah. Um, I don't have words for this.

I mean it's incredible we live in a day and age where the pharmaceutical companies can do just about whatever they want, say whatever they want on commercials, because so many Americans either need these meds, and/or have been convinced and brainwashed into believing they need these meds.

Let's just repeat that, it's a little baffling to hear at first. Antidepressant commercials and non-antidepressant commercials actually list "thoughts of suicide." as a side effect of the medications. The thing that is supposed to be helping you is causing you to want to kill yourself.

It's strange that I even have to say this, I mean am I crazy? Something seems wrong with this picture to me.

Don't anyone try to THINK about this for a second. The very drugs the pharmaceutical companies developed to be aids to subduing depression and suicide are actually drugs that can not only harm you but increase the probabilities of suicide. Seems to me the psychiatrists, clinical counselors, and pharmaceutical companies would rather kill us than cure us.

That's your cue to THINK about it by the way.

Over time I started to notice the effects of the meds in my body. I noticed when I was in high school, running Cross Country, that my body heat would rise beyond the norm, and I would feel very itchy for no reason. I'd often scratch my skin all over my torso to the point where my friends could see the pink marks from my nails. They'd ask me, "Did you get mauled by a bear?"

I just told them, "I get itchy when I run."

Now, at the time, I had no idea that this was actually a side effect of the meds. I didn't think it was anything. It was a precursor to something far worse later on.

I explained before that other side effects included feeling empty, numb; not happy, nor sad. I felt like a zombie, neither living nor dead. Just there, floating like a log in the water.

I felt thoroughly exhausted in every capacity, physically, mentally, emotionally. It's important that you, my readers, understand I felt empty spiritually, even though God's protection was with me. I will explain this further in another chapter.

The meds made it so that I slept very badly at night. I felt very foggy and slow, lethargic. As I said, I couldn't stay awake in class.

I also wanted to point out that with all the turmoil that was going on in my life, as well as the heavy weighted side effects of these meds, it was only by God's Grace that I not only finished high school but passed.

WITHDRAWAL EFFECTS INCLUDED ANYWAY - HAVE FUN

My Cousin who also is my teacher began telling me with perseverance, I can beat the withdrawal. I was visiting him and my Dad at the time for five months. During a two-week period near the end of the visit, I weaned myself off the meds.

I first started experiencing withdrawal effects on the way back home to Ohio. My Cousin and Dad were driving me back, when I started to have an unusual feeling of hunger in my stomach as if I hadn't eaten all day. It was growling. I started to have strange electrical impulses through the nerves in my limbs. I felt these hot flashes in my legs and whole body. I was rubbing my legs at the time. It all felt rather disturbing and shocking.

The closer I got to home, the more anxious I was getting. When we finally got there, said our goodbyes, and parted ways, I broke down and cried my heart out because I didn't want to return to Ohio. Even though I was of legal age, I was still tethered to my Mom, my custodial parent; due to the legalities of the divorce decree.

They later told me that they also cried as they drove away. I, myself, couldn't stop for a long time. It felt like I was being crushed again. Now I had to adapt to an old environment once more, even though it was the same one I had just left. At this point, my Mom felt like a stranger.

And if she felt like a stranger upon my arrival home, then when was she not a stranger?

This would prove to be the most intense, destructive, and extremely difficult year I had ever lived with my Mom.

Although it seemed pointless at the time, there was purpose in my coming back. There were things to learn, and growth to be made. There was more for me to learn about my Mom, and myself, which I will discuss at length later.

In the first three to four months, things in my body started to take a turn for the worse. It really started to scare me, especially in my mind and emotions.

I noticed a withdrawal effect that really freaked me out at the time. I was starting to experience hair loss. I wasn't really doing anything to cause this. I would be scratching my head normally, and more hair fell out than usual. Not huge amounts, but enough for me to notice a difference.

Did the psychiatrists tell me that would happen? NOPE.

Over time, my hairline started to recede. Back then, I was awfully concerned about my looks, so this was particularly frightening. And it did not stop. It just kept on going until my body finally got over the drugs.

All the time, I felt like I was in the basket of a hot air balloon, but there was no balloon. This meant that I was falling, falling, falling, falling. With nowhere to land, the process continued. It was the whole emotional and mental

49

rollercoaster. It didn't make any sense. IT WAS THE DRUGS.

Also, for the most part, I stopped sweating; my body sweated very little. Meaning, my body no longer cooled itself down in a reasonable amount of time; it was long and drawn out.

My nervous system was shot. All thrown out of wack. This will come into play later on.

Probably the worst withdrawal effect I ever experienced was when my body would break out in these hives. Red blotches and red bumps, I would get severe itching, yet scratching would not alleviate the sensation, but only made it worse.

When I scratched one spot, it may have temporarily relieved that area, but then it would jump to every other point on my body. So, I would be chasing the itch all over my flesh.

Unless you have been through something like this, I cannot possibly convey to you the reality of the panic inducing feeling I experienced when I would see my flesh turning this abnormal bright red color right before my eyes. It took no time at all for my skin and inner body to inflame.

The second part of this was the fiery burning sensation I experienced all over where these red blotches appeared and didn't appear. It felt like my nerves were on fire from the inside, and there was almost nothing I could do to cool down except drink something cold and douse my whole body in cold water.

I felt this particularly in my torso, in the small of my back, my spine, where a lot of nerves are housed. My chest, my arms, everywhere. My head too. My forehead, my scalp. Scratching my scalp would just make the hair fly, ripping hair out of my head.

I believed, at the time, that the roots of the hair on my head had grown weaker because of the drugs. So, they were dislodged much easier from scratching.

The third part of this goes back to when I said my nervous system was shot. It felt like everything caused a heat/hives reaction. My anxiety, my emotions, particularly anger and fear caused the previously stated physical reactions. Emotions are directly connected to and affect the nervous system, so it makes sense that they would trigger these unstable drug induced physical abnormalities. The effects of all this caused my mind to be convinced there was no way out.

The fourth part was that heat was also a major trigger to these reactions. I couldn't have hot drinks anymore. I couldn't take hot baths or hot showers. I couldn't even go outside in the hot sun. Yes, I was allergic to the sun. A real-life vampire. I couldn't stand it. I couldn't even sit outside for a few minutes without feeling something. Five minutes was all I could stand without suffering terribly.

I need to emphasize to you just how shocking this felt for me at the time. When I was sitting outside, knowing that in moments or minutes I was going to have a reaction, that can make you feel like a cripple. All these withdrawal effects can make you feel like a cripple. You feel like

51

there's nothing you can do to stop them; you have no control.

You are in pure anxiousness and fear of what you know is coming. I cannot put into words just how scary this all felt internally. If I was not careful, my mind could create the heat/hives prematurely. That's how powerful the mind can be.

I was hurt to the core, heartbroken, and filled with explosive infuriating rage, by the fact that neither my family, nor my doctors believed me. I was told by the medical profession that I was delusional. I could see it in their faces as well as my family's faces. They all thought I was crazy. Doesn't that show just how stark raving mad the medical professionals were and are today? The very people who prescribed me the stuff were telling me I'm delusional based on the effects of these medications. That means that they have zero understanding of what the meds can actually do. I was a real-life example of their work coming back to them, and they flat out refused to see it.

My Mom's insensitive actions proved to me that she did not believe me. That was evident by the fact that no matter how many times I explained to her what was happening, particularly the triggers, such as her emotional outbursts directed at me, she did not listen and kept up her antics. Because of this, she kept triggering these withdrawal effects and alienating me even further. That pushed me to hate her more.

Many months into my withdrawal, one of my siblings said to me I shouldn't be experiencing this anymore. My sibling actually had the nerve, no pun intended, to tell me that I should be over this. It was as though everyone in my family thought they knew my body better than me. That was the kind of psycho circus I was living in, the kind of people I was surrounded by. The ones who were closest to me, yet the furthest apart.

I'm not making this up. These were real triggers that instantly caused this physical reaction in my body. I did not create this with my mind. The drugs did.

I know some people may have a hard time believing this is possible, but this is reality. These things happen all the time to people. The pharmaceutical companies just don't want you to know it, and they cover it up. The psychiatrists cover it up. How would they make money otherwise?

I went through three years of this withdrawal drug hell. Three years of excruciating burning pain. And if you still have a hard time believing this is true, then let me say this. Everything single withdrawal effect that I just described is directly connected to the nervous system. Think back a few chapters to the Cleveland Clinic's definition of serotonin.

SOCIAL ANXIETIES

My traumatic experiences crippled my ability to relate to people, or at the very least, buried it beneath a deep amount of emotional and mental turmoil. I seemed to become a completely different person over a short amount of time. My identity seemed to be lost, I was not who I was anymore. And that hurt more than I can say. The most horrible feeling was that I didn't know how to fix it, therefore no matter how I tried to fix it, nothing would work. I felt helpless, broken inside.

I acted out many times, became a loudmouth; I was angry with people because they were horrible to me, therefore I fought them. Suddenly it felt like there was all this hostility against me, as if my reality had turned against me, many people around me seemed to become bitter, and those who didn't, did not seem to notice me. Even though I had been hurting at school, and bad things happened to me there, the grand foundation of this pain came from the extreme neglect of my parents and family.

One thing my Cousin explained to me was that God redirected people away from me, and that saved me more pain and suffering. He also told me that people did admire me, did respect me, but many didn't have the courage to approach me. They did see how good I was. I don't believe they saw my depth, but perhaps a measure of my goodness.

One thing I've learned after all these years is that I was simply different from everyone around me where I grew up, family included. That depth of goodness at the center of my heart was what set me apart. And I was surrounded by generally superficial and heartless people; people who were ruled by their minds. Since it seemed there was no one like me, I felt hurt by everyone and everything. I was like a diamond in a field of mud. The problem was that I didn't and couldn't see my own luster, see my own worth. I couldn't understand why I hurt so badly.

The truth was that my classmates did admire me from a distance, but for a multitude of reasons they did not approach me. Anger, fear, no matter the reason. I'm sure many of them had their own turmoil going on in their lives which may have made them oblivious to what was happening in others' lives around them. Abandonment occurred as a result of me not understanding actions taken.

I had convinced myself that everyone was against me, teachers, students, and worst of all family. The negative power of my mind created arenas of nothingness. In one arena, I became convinced I had no social skills. Thus, when attempting to interact with classmates, oft times they looked at me as though I was an alien from outer space. I felt guilty for my lack of social skills, while, in reality, nothing was wrong with me; I believed everyone thought I was stupid.

Awkwardness and anxiety were another arena I had to deal with. Because of this, it triggered the overheated body, red splashes on the skin, and sporadic breathing.

I want people to understand the thought processes that were channeled through my mind when interacting with people. I felt awkward, out of place, like the synapses in my brain were not connecting or flowing, therefore I felt like my social interactions were equally not connecting or flowing.

Foundationally, I could not build upon anything firm. When most of my peer group were going to dances, movies, hanging out at the mall, or just attending a house party, fear kept me from participating.

I need you parents who are reading this to understand, if you push your child into a corner, the walls that they build up will shut you out as well. The road to recovery will not include trying to force classmates and friends on your child. For his or her own protection, they have neatly ERECTED a box around themselves and nobody is getting in, AND THEY'RE NOT COMING OUT.

SUICIDE

At this stage I was overwhelmed physically, mentally, emotionally, and spiritually. I remember being in a computer room at school in the last period of the day. That's when I was looking at what was around me; the people, my classmates, my teacher, the world around me, and it all just sickened me. I hated everything and everyone around me.

To me, these were not people. They walked carelessly throughout their day, thoughts of helping others far from their minds, no thought of helping me. This was why I hated that school so much, because of the emptiness of it, the heartlessness of the students and staff around me. There was nothing my friends could do to help me; we couldn't be further apart; they didn't know me anymore; therefore, they were useless to me.

And my family might as well have lived on the moon. Space was where they lived. And that may have been the most painful thing at the time. That my own family, my loved ones who I had known from the start were nowhere to be seen in my most desperate hour. I was absolutely, unequivocally, irrevocably alone.

It was like I was in some desert hellscape, dust flying in clouds off the ground, the sun barely visible through a haze. The land was dead and barren. And somehow, I had ended up here, walking through pandemonium.

I cannot emphasize how wrong it is for parents not to be present at a time like this in their child's life. I promise you with all my heart that if you mistreat your children, or simply neglect them in every way that they need you, then this is where they will end up. Dead. And the blood will be on your hands.

To my parental readers, you want to know what dying feels like? WELL, THIS IS IT. And you should be grateful to have FRONT ROW CENTER SEATS. Not everyone has the strength or the wisdom enough to open their hearts to the world and share their sad stories; all in the attempt to make sure that NO ONE ELSE DIES BECAUSE OF YOUR FAILURES AS PARENTS. Don't be getting angry at me for telling the truth. YOU NEEDED TO HEAR THAT. Whether you like it or not, I am here to help you.

Anxiety, pressure, uselessness and anger. For twenty-four hours a day, seven days a week, this was my life. Too many times my thought process was to end my life, to cause these things to stop happening. Again, as I forestated, not my parents, my siblings, my teachers, nor my friends knew the darkness that was looming over me. That, my readers, is a sad state of affairs. Even sadder, my dog was a better friend to me than anybody. On a professional note, my psychiatrist and my clinical counselor only scratched the surface, and just drugged me up. So, who could I confide in when everybody in my life was clueless and non-accepting of my reality? That fact alone can make a person believe everyone around him is bat-doo-doo crazy, and inspire absolute hatred for them, and rightfully so. Because at that point, they have absolutely failed him or her.

As I was saying earlier, by the time the end of the school day was upon me, I was fed up, full of emotion, and had resigned myself there was no way out. I wanted all of this to end. And the only way I could think of to make that happen was to end my life. It seemed like a far greater peace at the time than to continue onward through the muck and mire of this drained existence, where I felt unwanted and that there was no one to help me.

I thought about how I would commit the act on the walk home. An idea crossed my mind to try to get a hold of a family member's handgun and blow my brains out. After some thought, I decided that was too complicated. I had a flip-blade in my room at home, that seemed much simpler. So, when I got home, I went up to my room, got the knife, sat at my desk, and got ready to check out.

Here is the difficult part.

All my life had led to this moment; this experience which I would learn immeasurable wisdom from; this experience that would help to shape my life for all coming days.

I opened the blade and held it in my left hand, I exposed the underside of my right wrist and brought the edge of the knife down upon it. My mind and emotions were awash with wildfire, my thoughts twisted and turned around all the things that tormented me. My emotions were white-hot and self-destructive. I hated myself, I felt so weak.

My life was ending and beginning. Such strife and suffering had led to this moment, and I didn't know how I got through it at the time. The blade was cold as it bit down into my wrist, but no matter how hard I tried to rend my flesh and end my life, something was pushing back against me.

For several long minutes, I sat there trying to push the blade down, but through my sobbing and extreme frustration, I was unable to harm myself. I couldn't bring myself to do it, and I didn't know why. I chose to live. And because then, I knew that I had no easy way out, I just sobbed and sobbed and cried my heart out. Because reality was setting in that I was going to have to take what seemed like the impossible path forward. Life.

Now I know exactly why I was spared. God had saved my life from destruction when no one else would. God and his protective angels bolstered my remaining love for myself and that was what was pushing back against me. They made it unbreakable, so I couldn't have overpowered God even if I had tried.

So that was the end of that. I wouldn't be using all the wisdom that I had learned to write this book if God hadn't saved my life that day.

Unfortunately, even though I was alive, my life was about to get a whole lot darker.

THE PSYCH WARD

I want to begin this chapter by recognizing the honesty and trust that young people possess at the beginning of their lives. They're more innocent. There is honesty and trust, particularly for parents and family.

After my suicide attempt, I felt happy that I was alive and I took this happiness to my Mom, trusting in her to be understanding. I had a quality of being honest with my family because they were the ones that I was supposed to be able to depend on for anything.

So, I told my Mom what happened and held nothing back. Not everyone who goes through suicide attempts would do this. In fact, more often than not, they wouldn't. But I did. That should go to show how much trust I had in my family, as it should be. And what came next revealed how they broke that trust and my heart with it. And then they would go on living like nothing was wrong.

My Mom had the polar-opposite response than I expected. She freaked out completely and called my clinical counselor, who scheduled an emergency meeting with us. I told my Mom beforehand that I was okay, that I had chosen to live. That should have been enough for her, but sadly it was not.

We went and talked with my clinical counselor who was also having an adverse reaction. He was suggesting to my Mom to throw me in the psych ward because he said, and I quote, "I would feel safer if you were in the psych ward overnight." So, this wasn't about me anymore, it was about him feeling safe in his professional position. And I told him the same thing I told my Mom, that I was okay and had chosen to live. Not enough for him. My Mom went with the opinion of the professional instead of listening to me.

I remember the look in her eyes, the conflict. I was looking at her beside me on the couch like, *Are you going to let him do this?* And what do you know? She let him do it. Off to the psych ward I went. YAY.

We went to a hospital first, where I was put on a stretcher in an ambulance and taken to a different hospital, then up to the adolescent psych ward in the middle of the night when no one was awake. That was God protecting me that no crazy people were awake at the time, or I might have lost it.

I remember a blond nurse who escorted us to my new room, which had a large window of a great view overlooking a bridge. It was the most humiliating feeling, giving up all your clothes and possessions, having them search you for weapons that you would use to kill yourself or anybody else with.

I cannot emphasize just how wronged I felt in my heart; it was like an unbearable heat emanating from my chest. I could feel it in every breath as it burned through my eyes as I stared at my Mom with absolute hatred. Feeling like, *How could you have done this to me?* And I could see it in her eyes, she knew she was guilty, but clueless as to how to help me. Instead, she would just leave it to others. I remember telling her that I didn't want my siblings to come and visit me. I didn't want them to see me like this.

That first night I had a lot of hot tears, coldness, and emptiness. I felt like an empty husk that had been abandoned by its family yet again, to the underbelly of psychotic hell.

Know this. Until you have been treated like a nutcase, strapped to a stretcher, hauled off to a psychiatric ward in a hospital somewhere, then stripped of your clothes, given a gown, searched for weapons, and generally just treated like an animal, you have no idea whatsoever how humiliating that is. And with the permission of your own parent no less. It's like betrayal, having your heart ripped out of your chest. You then watch your heart set ablaze by your own hatred.

During the night, the nurse would come in to check on me. They had to keep a constant watch, I'm sure. I kept closing the door because they kept leaving it open when they left. I just wanted privacy.

The next day I spent in my room. I didn't come out to see anyone or meet any of the other kids, not like there were that many.

The second day was when the nurse encouraged me to come have breakfast with everyone. I got to meet the crazy people and the normal people that the state and government love to lump into the same bucket together, when there is absolutely no reason to.

I didn't say much. It wasn't so bad, but some of the kids really did need to be there. Others were fine and didn't need to be there. Some of them were thrown in there by their families, same as I was.

After eating, I went back to my room. The nurse came and told me they were having school, but I refused to go. As the days went on, I began to open up little by little, interacted with the other kids more, established a little comfort.

I had to go and see the psychiatrist in the psych ward who regulated my meds, to change some meds according to how I was feeling.

I did learn some things in there, like how insensitive some parents are to their children, to their own family. There was this extremely scrawny kid who had come in overnight. He looked like he hadn't been eating for a while. His parents were sitting on either side of him in the dining room with all of us. He still wasn't touching his plate, but simply staring down at it with empty eyes. His parents kept on telling him he needed to eat something again and again like that was all they knew to say. I could tell very quickly that they didn't know how to handle him. They were as clueless on how to take care of their children as other parents are.

I could feel the tension building in the atmosphere. I could feel his resistance to them, and their incessant pressing nature on him. What complicated the problem was a girl, who was a psych patient, sitting on the other side of his mother. A girl I knew to be crazy. She pointed at the scrawny kid's food tray, and actually asked him, "Are you going to eat that?" At the time, I couldn't believe she was asking him that. It only added fuel to the fire, especially when she reached over with her fork to try and take something off his tray. Now I was trying to get her attention to divert her from him. She looked at me, but clearly didn't or couldn't receive the message.

The mother noticed and tried to push the fork away. Meanwhile, all these factors compounded, and the kid had a complete psychotic breakdown. He just kept repeating and stuttering, "I need… I need to kill myself." Endlessly he said this, and nurses came in to calm the situation. The parents looked on cluelessly and with shock.

I was a bit shocked too. I got up and left. I went in the bathroom inside my room and just stayed in there for a while. I leaned against the door and slid down to the floor, taking in the whole crazy situation that had just occurred. That was by far the most insane experience I had there. All of that never would have happened if those parents hadn't so stupidly handled the situation. Whether or not they realized it, they drove him to have a psychotic episode.

Other than my Mom visiting me a couple times, there isn't much else to say. It was crazy, no pun intended. Finally, after some time, I was allowed to leave and my Mom took me home. And it was over for now…

The last thing I remember was when I was walking out to my freedom, with a smile on my face. As I passed the dining room on my left, I glanced over at some of the normal friends I had made, and they looked disappointed, as though to ask, *Why are you leaving us here?*

Why are you leaving us here? That is a look that I am sure is in the eyes of a lot of children when they gaze at their parents. The parents are just too blind to see it.

It was only five months later that I had a second breakdown and subsequent suicide attempt, after which the same set of circumstances ensued. My Mom freaked out, so she and my clinical counselor once again threw me to the wolves. This time I was no longer an adolescent. I had turned eighteen, so I was placed in an adult psych ward. And man, there were some crazy people in there that I had tense run ins with.

I had my school bag with me when I was admitted, and I had totally forgotten that there was a lighter buried at the bottom of my bag. Let me be clear, truthfully, I did not know that it was in there. I was also drug tested when I was brought in, and just as I expected, I popped positive for marijuana.

Partway through my stay I was taken to a small class about drug use. It was me, a middle-aged gentleman, and a teacher. I was told that a lighter had been found in my school bag. Strangely, however, they did not, I repeat, not address my marijuana usage. And this is a class about drug use. No comment.

I told them the truth. I didn't know the lighter was in there, but they went on not believing me, most likely believing I was just another drug addict who lies and lies to cover up.

The older gentleman in the class with me was a coke addict. So, the reasons as to why they lumped me into a class with him can only be that my Mom or clinical counselor or both told them I was a marijuana user. Allow me to make clear that I was a casual user. I never smoked it anywhere near as much as the potheads I was surrounded by at school. The only reason I turned to it was out of my suffering. I do not condone its use when you are depressed. It will only enhance your depression. The initial high will turn to a low, and then it won't help you anymore.

Just like the first time I was in the adolescent psych ward, I told my Mom again that I didn't want my siblings to visit me there. I did not want them to see me like that.

My experiences in the psych wards offered me the very incredible reality of just how screwed up the system is and how desperately it needs to change. They take insane people and sane people and dump them all together in the same bucket. That in essence, is what a psych ward is, a bucket to dump all the undesirables.

But who cares, right? As long as the children and adults can stay drugged up and housed in the wards, then people can continue getting paid. It's a lovely system. And as long as no one with a heart emerges, who is ready and willing to go on a full-frontal assault against the medical institutions of the United States of America, and willing to sacrifice all, then nothing is going to change. And since I don't see anyone doing that, this is what we have right now.

So, in hindsight I was just another victim of a corrupt system, whose parents did not protect him from that system. Wow. Sounds just like millions of other children and adults in this country.

This was the beginning of the end of any trust I had left for my family.

CLINICAL COUNSELOR'S CHARACTER

You can learn a lot about people based on what they say, do, and think. This is a skill that is learned through experience. I used to not be very perceptive of this, but now I have learned much about my past based on what I know now.

It's important for me to note how my clinical counselor responded to my experiences inside the psych ward, because they reveal much about his true nature.

When I told him about the anorexic patient who wanted to kill himself, my counselor had this pleased expression on his face. Then he said something along the lines of, "Puts things in perspective, doesn't it?"

This was very wrong because he was hoping to hear that I had bad experiences in there, so that it would scare me away from death, even if it traumatized me. He was not thinking about the harmful effects these experiences would have on me. I know now that this was part of why he authorized me being put in there.

Let's also reiterate that he plainly said, "I would feel safer if you were in the psych ward overnight."

Rewind that. He said, "I would feel safer." IT WAS ABOUT HIM, HOW HE FELT. NOT ABOUT HOW I FELT. My free will and well-being were not even in the picture here for my Mom and counselor. THEY JUST STEAM ROLLED OVER THE FACT THAT I CHOSE TO LIVE.

WHAT IS SO HARD TO SEE ABOUT THAT?

This is where a lot of parents, clinical counselors, therapists, psychiatrists, psychologists, but especially parents, fail. Because they're not thinking about the child, they're thinking about themselves. Some of them don't even know that they're doing this. Conversely, some of them ARE AWARE they're doing this.

It should be said that this is not a man of God. This is a man of science and ego. The cornerstone of why many medical professionals fail. Science alone cannot solve everyone's problems.

Science failed me. God saved my life, not a clinical counselor or a psychiatrist. I know that there is a whole gigantic mentally deficient movement in this country that tries to suppress or destroy any kind of belief in God or angels. But God is real. I would be providing three square meals and dessert for the worms and dirt microorganisms without God. And you would not be reading this book right now if God had not saved my life. I'm sick of people who constantly try to say God is not real, and they rely completely on science to save them.

Allow me to paint a very clear picture. My parents did not protect me. My school was making the desire to live more difficult. Can you imagine the sadness in my heart when I realized I was invisible to my family? And the life was draining from me more and more through every experience. I had no one to save me. Literally I had no one, not one true friend, or legal guardian who was really looking out for my best interests.

How did I survive? How could I have possibly survived that? The only answer is God.

69

It's God that saved my life. Saved me from destruction, saved me from death. And that was probably the hardest thing I ever had to do in my life, choosing the harder path, choosing to live, choosing not to take the easy way out and die. God wasn't going to let me die. It was not my time. There was still so much for me to do on this earth. One of those tasks was for me to write this book, share my experiences with people so that they may live, heal, and follow God.

My clinical counselor tried to get me to accept that there is no God, and if I had chosen to listen to him, then I would most certainly be dead right now.

This is also an example of a man who relies on his own strength to get through this life. What a lonely life that must be, but not to him. He convinced himself that he is happy, safe, and secure in his own delusions.

In my clinical counselor's mind, he fulfilled the American dream. Nice family, nice car, nice home. But from his lofty perch, he still could not see God, or see God carrying me.

There is only one relatively comfortable way through this life, and that is with you following God. Remember that God doesn't take sides, contrary to what many fools have uttered in war. You are either on His side, or you are not. You have to choose Him. You have to choose a life of God over your own foolishness.

You have to choose to believe the things that seem impossible or unbelievable or unachievable. Why is it so hard to believe that God will provide for you? That He will give you all the things you need and fulfill the desires of your heart. House, car, bills taken care of, steady job.

70

Belonging, the need for love and a family, true friends, brothers or sisters. You need parents? He's got them for you. All you have to do is believe in Him and be patient. It will all come in due time.

My clinical counselor, this was also the man who talked about nurse's tits and told me on the phone to enjoy the eye candy when I was in my second psych ward experience. That should sum up the world of science and medical expertise right there. Tits.

AMERICA THE BEAUTIFUL? AMERICA THE DRUG HELL

One freakish withdrawal effect I had was that I lost twenty pounds in one month as a result of discontinuing my enslavement to these meds, courtesy of corporate pharmaceutical overlords of America, and their psychiatric and psychological sidekicks. I'd like to point out the very interesting fact that the root word of psychiatrist and psychologist is psyche, from which we get psycho. That should tell you something about who they really are.

Had I resisted the psych ward, they would have shot me up with drugs, restrained me like I was some criminal, and dragged me off to psycho hell. Joy joy, right? And until you've been through something like that, you have no idea what it's like. When your heart is broken, your mind has a hole in it based on your experiences. When you feel your family has abandoned and betrayed you, and you're shipped off to a place where people are truly unhinged in an atmosphere of madness, that is the worst kind of hell I can imagine. And I can do better than imagine it, I lived it.

Plus, there's always a chance that they can pump you so full of drugs to make sure you calm down. What they call calming you down is what I call being transformed into a drooling drug zombie, where you can't talk, can't walk, can't think. They have made you a prisoner in your own mind to keep you under control. That could be the story of the rest of your life if they had their way. It's worse than slavery. It's silent murder. Erasing your identity. And the loveliest part about all this is that it's completely legal. This is America. The land of greed and the home of the pharmaceutical drug psychos. Thank God I had the wisdom not to physically resist but go willingly to the psych ward. It could have been a very different story if I had resisted.

I was also thankful to God for delivering me to the milder psych wards, and not to places that could have caused me true psychological, physical, emotional, and spiritual harm. I didn't need to be broken any more than I already was. So, God spared me that. The ironic thing about all this is that my Grandfather worked for a pharmaceutical company. Poison was being pumped into my veins by companies like the one my Grandfather worked for.

One of the greatest things I can say about the pharmaceutical companies is the level of gratitude that they have inspired in me. I want to thank you, the pharmaceutical companies, from the deepest recesses of my heart, from the depths of my soul, for giving me the tools to bring about your total, complete, inevitable, undeniable, unalterable, and absolute destruction. The best part about all this, the part I take particular joy in, is that I didn't have to do anything. You did this. You did this to yourselves. The second you put that murderous poison into my veins, you created this book. The second you put that toxin into my blood, you destroyed yourselves. See how that works? That's what we call bad karma. That's what we call EVIL. I know it's a foreign concept and a big word to people like you. So, sound it out with me. EEEEE - VVVVV - IIIII - LLLLL. What does that spell?

EVIL - profoundly immoral and wicked.

"his evil deeds"

"the pharmaceutical companies innumerable evil deeds in drugging up half or more of the children and adults in America. Congratulations. Here is your ticket to hell. Enjoy."

How many people have you killed? Or at the very least helped to kill? What? You don't believe you did that? You don't believe you committed these evil deeds? Then tell that to the mountains and foundations of dead bodies of the people who were unable to get off these medications because you and the psychoanalytical people you are in bed with impressed upon them that they would be on these medications for the rest of their lives. How many of them died depressed believing your medications might or would save them? How many of them fought, and clawed, and bled their way through life only to realize that the miracle poison you had prescribed them DOES NOT WORK. And then they took their own lives. Or in my demographic, the people who attempted suicide and failed.

Whether or not you realize it, whether or not you believe it, whether or not you accept it, the ocean of blood imparted by those bodies, by those lives, by those human lives, by children, by men, by women, fathers and mothers, sons and daughters, cousins, aunts and uncles, grandfathers and grandmothers and grandchildren and so on, all that blood is on your heads, your hands, your bodies, your entire beings. That blood is you. It's the sum measure and cost of your life spent addicting people to these medications. Can't you feel that weight pressing down on you? Aren't you tired? Or have you simply fooled yourself into believing it doesn't exist?

Well, wherever your insane minds, in need of these medications are, know that there is a price to pay for these sins. And the price, in part, is this book, where I tell the truth to the world. I speak up for the people too afraid to talk about this beyond-urgent-issue. This matter of life and death. The great thing about the truth is that there is nothing you can do to stop it. No obscene amounts of money you can throw at its transparent essence. There is no way that you can burn it or destroy it in any way. There is nothing you can do to stop it from having its light in the open. Sure, you can delay it as best as possible, but one day, sooner or later, it will always find its way out. The more you try to strangle it, to stifle and suppress it, the stronger it will become until it overwhelms you. So, you've got to be one special kind of stupid person to fight it.

Thank you again, the pharmaceutical companies and psychoanalytical world, for giving me the tools for your destruction. Thank you for putting me through the hellfire that would ultimately forge this book to transform the world. For this I bless you.

THE BOOK OF DEATH AND DYING

After being given several weeks off, I finally returned to school after my first suicide experience. All my teachers had been briefed on what happened to me. In one of my classes, the teacher with no pre-collaboration or warning decided to put me on the spot in front of my classmates. This was what was requested of me. "I want you to share with the class what happened to you." All at once, my body heated up, my palms became really sweaty, and I physically tensed up with great pressure. I couldn't believe he had just done that. All eyes were on me with baited, glaring, and expressionless faces. Deep inside I knew I was not about to share my experiences with anybody. One good thing that resulted from my clinical counselor was the fact he instilled in me that I never had to talk about this with anyone. He instructed me to use these words, "I just wasn't feeling well. That's all."

Not satisfied with my response, a few minutes later, the teacher again pushed me to open up to my fellow students, and they got the same response as before. Later when class was dismissed, my teacher caught up with me in the hall and hugged me, as if conveying his affection where he had absolutely failed with his words. Quite frankly, I neither wanted nor needed a hug from the likes of a person such as this. The next year, I dropped his class because I could not see myself trying to interact with an insensitive buffoon.

One day, not long after this bizarre encounter, my teacher handed out a load of different books to the entire class, tailored to each student by him. He was giving them to us for free; we were to take them home. The book that was plopped down on my desk was called, 'Death and Dying'.

After a minute or so of staring at it, wondering if this was some kind of sick joke, I picked up the book and dropped it on another desk, trading it for a different book. And apparently, my teacher noticed this, because a minute or two later, he came by and got the book, and dropped it back on my desk.

At this point I knew for sure that he wanted me to read it. I don't know what you, my readers, may think about this, but personally, I find it insensitive, unprofessional and utterly ridiculous for a teacher to give a student who has just gone through suicide, a book about death and dying. But that's just me. That's like going up to a person who recently had their arm amputated, has no prosthetic yet, and asking them to carry a bag of groceries.

To this day, I don't know the purpose of the teacher giving me the book, nor have I read it. The insensitivity and callous nature of this person drew a definite wedge between us.

In retrospect, I now realize that because of my unwillingness to share my experience with my classmates, this teacher unjustifiably presented me with that book. Let me make this clear. At no time was I approached and asked in private if I would like to share my experience with my classmates. Nor was I forewarned that I was to be the center of attraction in discussing my suicide attempt. Needless to say, my "hate-o-meter" rose to an all level new high. If the man doubled over choking, I would have just watched him die.

COMPUTER SCHOOL

My breakdown didn't just happen in the blink of an eye. It was a constant process over the course of my four years in high school. It was in the last two years that I began to drop classes, especially advanced ones that had become too cumbersome for me to bear. It was in my junior year that I had a particularly inflammatory experience with my music class.

One of the classes I ended up dropping was symphonic band/marching band. And I remember telling my band director that I didn't want him to declare to the class that I was leaving. We seemed to have an agreement on this. And what did he do? This man publicly declared in front of everyone that I was leaving, and I was sitting right there in class watching him do this. He made this announcement when I had specifically told him I didn't want people to know in that way. If my classmates had come to me between classes and asked me about it one on one, then that would have been easier to handle. BUT NOT ALL IN ONE KNOCK OUT PUNCH. IT WAS LIKE HE WAS STICKING A FLAMING DAGGER IN MY HEART. It was at this moment that I had more than a few classmates looking at me like I was a traitor. You've got to remember that at this point I didn't have much fight left, I couldn't handle this kind of ignorant crap anymore.

My readers, this should go to show you how some folks (my band teacher) live in their own little fantasy worlds where they hear you say one thing, but don't listen to the words coming out of your mouth. They hear one thing and interpret it through their own convoluted ways of thinking. They're not processing correctly what you are saying, or even worse, they don't want to. They act like idiots and make stupid decisions. Then you are the one who pays for it. That was one of the worst experiences I had in dropping classes.

I was dying a little bit more each day at school. It seemed as if the days were growing more and more difficult, as if weights were strapped to my legs, and they were only getting heavier with time. I couldn't handle it anymore. I couldn't keep the mask on my face anymore. I couldn't keep the act up in front of people anymore, hiding my suffering. I had done it for too long. Far too long. Readers, don't you think that after you have a suicidal ordeal, when you return to school it should be easier, not harder? And if it's harder, that's because the idiots around you are making it harder.

I talked to my guidance counselor at school. She was one of four people managing almost two thousand students, so naturally she was not going to care. At least not to the extent of understanding, or of meeting my needs. Over the course of some months, she helped me out of several classes that I simply couldn't keep up with anymore. As I said, my strength was flagging, and my flame was burning low. She helped me to drop them one at a time.

Amazingly, my guidance counselor filled one of my more difficult classes that I had dropped with a men's choir class. I couldn't believe she had done this at first. After everything I had just gone through to get out of the spotlight, she was throwing me right back into it. How ignorant can you be? Answer me this simple question, my readers. After you've had a brush with suicide, do you really think you're going to want to sing in a choir? Are you stupid? That still leaves me dumbfounded to this day.

Now at the time, I was in a state of mind where I didn't think I had a choice in the matter. But after doing the choir class for a number of weeks, and with things continuing to spiral down for me at school, I went with my Mom to speak with my guidance counselor. My counselor spoke with us about a small school where I could finish out my classes on the computer. I agreed to this idea, and she talked to the principal. He wholeheartedly agreed and approved my transfer to this place. It was a mountainous sigh of relief for me, and I wouldn't realize until later that this was a God ordained miracle. It saved me by taking the pressure off, stripping the weights from my legs. Over the years I went to my high school, I never really talked to my principal. He seemed like an okay guy, cordial, and with nice manners. He would often walk through the cafeteria eating an apple, saying hello to everyone with a nice big smile. But it wasn't until this day that I realized he was a good man with a good heart. I give him great credit for doing this, because he sure didn't have to. This should also prove to you, my readers, that God places the right people in the right places at the right time to make critical differences in your life.

And the results of my going to this school were wonderful. I didn't have to get up at the crack of dawn anymore, a feat that was already difficult given the fact I was on medications that made it hard to stay awake anyway.

It was only three hours a day, as opposed to the usual seven hours at public school. And as for the work, basically you did as much as you could possibly do in a single day. There was no rush, no pressure, no insanity, no bullying, no fears, no anxiety, no stress, no crushing weight of an atmosphere of thousands of people around me all day long. Just me and a computer that I had to stare at and solve problems on. I finished what school subjects remained for me in my senior year, and I was done in a matter of four or five months. I completed my schooling months before my classmates did at the high school.

And then I was done with school. Just like that it was all over. Right?

JUDGED AND SUFFOCATED - PART 1

I need to get the point across about my family's way of not accepting who I was, what I was, how I was. To this day they still do not know who I am because I never felt safe enough to be myself around them. They were all so different, like a different breed altogether, or cut from a different cloth.

What I mean is, I couldn't talk about what I liked or enjoyed without being judged. They didn't like just about anything that I liked. There was no relating to them on any level.

To give you an example, I was afraid of being seen watching the same movie again and again from time to time because they judged me for it. They didn't always have to say it, I knew they were thinking it. I could see it on their faces.

They judged me for my fantasy interests, for example medieval fiction novels, sci-fi novels, all that stuff. They thought I lived in fantasy land. One of my siblings convinced my Mom that I played video games too much. But you see, video games were a good escape and therapy for me at the time, because every day was hell. Video games were perhaps one of the only things that I enjoyed doing, maybe the only thing. They sure did a better job at keeping me alive than paying sixty dollars a visit to a clinical counselor who would just fill my head with lies and all manner of nonsense. Video games were the only time during the day when I felt peace.

The point is that I could not be myself around them because of who they were, and I had no one to teach me any better. To teach me not to care about such malarkey.

It was slow suffocation for the whole beginning of my life. Each day spent around my family was like there was less oxygen. Only by God did I survive them and their insane convoluted ways. I want my readers out there who live in crazy families, who feel like they're just surviving their family's day to day, to know that they're not alone.

You are not crazy, no matter how much your family and everyone around you is trying to convince you that you are. You're not. If I was insane, how could I have written a book to help people? If you were insane, how could you have comprehended the message I'm sending you?

To me, it's the same way mountain climbers increasingly deal with asphyxia the higher they climb up a mountain. It gets to a point where they must use oxygen tanks to climb to the summit.

Well, my school, my classmates, my teachers, my friends, my psychiatrist, my clinical counselor, and especially my family all took the form of the asphyxia. Depriving me of oxygen. Only I wasn't going up a mountain. I was slipping beneath the waves of the ocean, sliding down the great mountain sized slopes of a continent, all the way to the rock bottom.

Only, my oxygen tanks were God himself, and I never would have made it out alive without God. He is my oxygen. Now I can breathe.

JUDGED AND SUFFOCATED - PART 2: NONACCEPTANCE

I'd like to expand on the reasons why I felt that my family would not accept me by providing a little evidence. It was simply in the way they acted. Trying to get my Mom and Dad to read some of my favorite fantasy novels was like pulling teeth. It took months, possibly years if I remember right.

When I tried to show Mom some sci-fi and/or fantasy TV shows and movies that struck me, it was the way she looked at me, her reactions to the material, her general atmosphere, and disinterest. Again, I reiterate, she thought I was living in fantasy land.

Now, my readers, I want you to consider how my truth would feel in this matter. The very subject that I loved, which by extension was a part of me, was being shown a general lack of care. In fact, it was being judged, and so was I. To further aid in my family's seeming distaste, my clinical counselor stated I have a problem with reality, and therefore live in fantasy land. This was the proverbial nail in the coffin.

My parents finally agreed to read one of my favorite book series. Though they did not complete it, they at least made the effort. This gave me temporary satisfaction, but it was satisfaction under the umbrella, "Ryan lives in fantasy land."

It felt like they didn't accept what I loved, and because they didn't accept what I loved, it felt like they didn't accept me. And look how wrong they all were. It was always a part of who I am.

FALLING TO HATRED

One of the things that must be said, my readers, is that even before I tried to kill myself, I had already started to grow in resentment and bitterness towards my family. It transformed entirely into flat out hatred. I came home every day from school and took a hot shower until the water turned cold. I would lay down in the tub and just cry, cry, cry my heart out.

At this point the suffering had reached such a palpable state that I couldn't help it anymore. I was suffering. There isn't any other way to say it. And these feelings had grown to a place where I held my family responsible.

My siblings acted ignorant. They were children, like me, still growing and changing. Children always treat each other with some level of cruelty when they're growing up. This is the way it is in every family. Children, my siblings for example, cannot be held accountable for my suffering. Their treatment must not be taken personally or allowed to fester later in life. At the time, though, I did not see it that way. They were all guilty in my eyesight.

But the real source of where the problem came from was my parents. Now, this was different than with siblings, because parents are the ones who are supposed to raise you strong. It's not the sibling's responsibility to raise you, therefore again, they cannot be held to account for your suffering.

Everything that had happened or did not happen between my parents and I was the root cause of my suffering. As a result, I began to harbor hatred for them. It eventually grew to a place where I wanted to kill them all. My parents and siblings included. I could not, for the life of me, understand why they were the way they were. Why they treated me the way they did. I felt this way because my definition of unconditional love was wholly and entirely different from their definition of unconditional love. Obviously, their definition of love was very skewed and misguided. I don't even think they knew what unconditional love was. They may have thought they knew, and I'm sure, in their minds, they saw nothing wrong with their definition, and nothing wrong with how they handled things with me, or anything in life for that matter.

But the thing that took me years to come terms with, to be honest with myself, was the fact that I had allowed myself to fall into this hellish place of burning emotion, thoughts of revenge slinking beneath the surface. At the same time, whether I knew it or not, there was still love for my family deep down. That was just the kind of unconditionally loving person I was. Love and hate cannot exist together; it felt as if there was this churning whirlpool of chaos and titanic conflict between love and hate inside me, ever pulling me this way and that, ripping me apart in their destructive tides. It would change how I felt many times. Some days when we were together as a family, I was

happy they were around; there were some rare positive moments and experiences, but then ultimately, inevitably, they would reveal to me their true nature once more and do something truly hurtful and stupid. Then I hated them again in an instant.

Let me say that I do not condone hatred. Hatred is wrong. There is no excuse for it. If you harbor it, I strongly suggest you work to rid yourself of such emotions and forgive whoever you perceive to be responsible for the wrongdoing, even if that person is yourself.

You've got to let the anger go. It's a poisonous cloud, a negative rock, a plague of negativity. You must ask the Lord to help you see through it, see beyond it, see the world without it. Otherwise, you are blind; you cannot see the light, you cannot see anything good. It's like looking through a negative lens. You have to change the lens.

I wouldn't learn until later in life that there was another reason that led to hatred for me. And that reason was that I was simply different from my family. Different down to the bone. Certainly, on an internal spiritual level. My siblings made different choices as to who and what they developed into. They went down paths that I would not, could not, and refused to follow. As they became increasingly crazier in my eyes, I became more distant from them. Because of this fundamental difference in our character, which I cannot entirely convey into words, hatred fostered due to the escalating sense that I did not belong, and could not fit in.

I believe now that God simply was not allowing me to go down those same paths they did, or that of the insane people at my school. He was not going to allow me to become tainted by the same impurities. He had other plans for me. I also believe that in a very real sense He kept me somewhat distant from my siblings because of their different nature. I didn't need that madness around me to

influence and change me into something I was not. He kept
me closer to who I am; protected the heart of me.

VIDEO GAMES

A few chapters back, I mentioned that I played video games. I did this pretty much every day right after school. It was my 'turn off' from a hellish cesspool of a reality of living death. It was a great and effective way for me to release all the craziness of my day. It was a way for me to focus my mind, to get my frustration, anger, and aggression out of my system, and on top of it all, it was fun.

As I said before, my family, particularly my Mom and one of my siblings, thought I lived in a fantasy reality. They just didn't understand me at all, not what I was facing, nor why I was playing video games. My sibling convinced my Mom that I played video games entirely too much; my Mom, who simply did not listen to me, and instead listened to everyone else on how to parent, everyone but herself (I must add), took up what my sibling was saying, and so, poured more painful pressure upon me to change. You see, my sibling had a way of making my life more of a living hell, and didn't even realize this, nor would said sibling have ever seen it that way.

The insane thing to me about my siblings, when dealing with our Mom, is that they knew exactly who she was and what she was capable of in her character. Yet when it came to my unbelievably ridiculous struggles with her, it was like they FORGOT ALL ABOUT WHAT SHE WAS LIKE. Instead, my siblings would automatically side with her, and go off what they heard from her about me.

As a result of what my sibling said to my Mom, she told my clinical counselor, who in turn believed as they did, that I was living in a fantasy world. This lead my Mom to not invest in my video game library, so I had very few games. Most of the games I had I bought myself. I bought the second controller myself, rechargeable battery packs myself, and I even bought the fifty-dollar option of Xbox Live for twelve months, myself. I really broke the bank for Xbox Live because of the conflicted attitude of my Mom, enhanced by the clinical counselor, and promoted by my sibling; and I accomplished this with no allowance.

Before all this, I didn't have any money to buy the Xbox with in the first place. At this stage of my life, everything I did or attempted to do had conditions. With my Mom, she would give me A, B, and C, as long as I did D, E, and F. With her, the mentality was 'I give you, you do for me.' Nothing was free, everything had a price attached to it. I had to mow the lawn just to get a burger from the drive through. When she bought me food, she would ask, "What are you going to do for me?" When she bought me clothes, she expected me to do some kind of work in return. This kind of behavior made me dread asking my Mom for anything.

Let me make it clear. I do believe that we have an obligation to aid around the house and keep up with chores. In my case, it was neither. So, I ended up feeling disillusioned and alienated from my Mom.

With this in mind, I had to paint six doors throughout the house, as well as our dining room, just so that my Mom would agree to buy the Xbox I wanted. By that math, I would have to build a house for her to buy me a car.

Since my Mom refused to buy me any games, and I felt I couldn't ask her for them, eventually this led to my selling the Xbox to someone I knew at school, eliminating one of the few things that I gained any kind of pleasure from.

I always thought parents were supposed to provide the basic needs for their children. I guess I was sadly mistaken. To you, my parental readers, please do not make the same mistake.

MAN'S BEST FRIEND

When I was young, maybe nine years old, my sisters said they'd come across a puppy that they wanted. I saw the picture that was taken of them holding it, and I remember thinking the dog was adorable. Our parents agreed to buy it, though I'm sure that in the back of my Dad's mind, he didn't want it. I really have no idea where my Mom's head was at back then. I think she just kind of went wherever the current was going.

I went with them to see the puppy and met its sister too. Both were cute, but we couldn't buy them both to keep the siblings together. There was even a three-legged dog and a blind dog, and these dogs could run really fast. I remember being struck by just how abnormally loveable our puppy was. Little did I know at the time just how strong a role this dog would play in the struggles of my later life.

It was a she and we named her Rory. Rory was a mongrel, a cross of different dog breeds, but the most prominent breed in her features was the Cocker Spaniel. She had those big ears, not as large as a traditional Cocker Spaniel, but large enough to know it was in her genetics. She was black and white, with a very unique and beautiful mark upon the crown of her head. A black spot inside a strip of white, surrounded by more black fur down the sides of her head. She was a very pretty dog. I used to say that she was a supermodel dog to my friends. When I walked her down the street, all the neighborhood dogs were howling from the windows of houses, because our dog was a diva.

Now, when the dog first came to us, it was a little thing. It had all the immature behavior and signs of a puppy that doesn't know what's what. A puppy, of course, is going to act up, do crazy things, even teethe and bite us, until we discipline that behavior out of it. I remember being afraid of it when it was in our house those first days. I'd never lived with a dog before. I remember one time, Rory wouldn't stop barking at me, chasing me, and I got up and sat on the table, with my legs on top of a chair, calling for help from my sister. This dog was feisty at first.

A puppy, just like a human baby, is going to need a lot of attention. So, in those first few nights, don't ask me why, but we had it inside of an old rabbit cage of ours. Rory was just mewling and barking and shrieking the whole night. And I remember that I had slept in my parent's bed that night, and my Dad got so pissed. You can imagine a man who takes everything as a personal attack, with mental and emotional instability, and how a noisy puppy is going to trigger that kind of man like a nuclear bomb going off. My Dad must have walked out of that room several times during the night, and slammed the top of that cage repeatedly, just to get the puppy to stop. He didn't comfort it, because I know he didn't care about it, nor did he even want it. This kind of snapping, impulsive, and emotionally uncontrolled behavior is the behavior of a child. These were also the last days of our family living all together in the same house. Soon after this, my Dad got out of the house, because he was going to go insane otherwise. Someone was going to die if he had not left.

Over the course of many years, as my turmoil increased and I was dying a little every day, Rory was a much-needed comfort for me at home. She became my best friend, my only real friend. Dogs are very loyal and loving to their owners, and Rory was a loyal dog. Sad to say, but my dog was more of a friend to me than my own family members; there was no comfort at school because my classmates could not measure up to even one quarter of my dog's love and devotion. Rory did not judge me or hound me over stupid things like how I was conducting my life. Rory did not attack me, nag me, or verbally assault me like some people did at school. Most of all, Rory did not treat me like I was some sick demented person who could not think for himself, nor did she insult my intelligence, or treat me like I was invisible on a daily basis. THE DOG SAW THAT I WAS THERE; THAT I WAS REAL. RORY DID NOT DENY MY EXISTENCE. I WILL REPEAT, MY DOG TREATED ME BETTER THAN MY FAMILY DID. What does that say about animals vs humans? We can learn a thing or two from them.

And you know the very interesting thing about Rory? She was very much neglected and left alone for the latter part of her life. I had to go to school, and Mom had to go to work all day, and didn't arrive home till after 5:00 PM. This dog had nothing to do all day until I arrived home to let her out. She would just sleep. I believed the dog got depressed. I know this because of all my siblings, and my Mom, I spent the most years around her. I knew her better than they did. My Mom was halfway or more clueless as to our dog.

The point I'm trying to make about my dog here is simple. Like me, she was neglected, left alone, treated almost like she was invisible, until she was just forgotten. Laying in her bed all day with no one around; kind of like how I slept in a bed or on a couch a lot, in a mental, emotional, and spiritual fog, induced by antidepressant medications.

So, the dog and I had a lot in common. I was all she had, and she was all I had. In this case she was 'Man's Best Friend,' or more accurately put, 'Man's Only Friend.'

DISRESPECT AND INVISIBILITY

One of the things that literally drove me into a crazed frenzy was the very fact that my family, Mom, Dad, siblings included, treated me with a dismissive disrespect. Nothing I did or said really got their attention. If I had jumped through hoops and breathed fire it still would not have gotten their attention. Do you know what it's like for everything you do and say to fall on complacent ears? It erodes you, makes you try ever harder to gain attention; you try to improve your techniques, your ways of being listened to. You become louder and crazier and desperate. There really aren't words to describe how messed up this nonsense is. It's your FAMILY. It's not supposed to be this complicated. But as forestated in this book, where dysfunctional, dismembered, and disoriented families abide, the chances of true family love are impossible.

I can still remember the looks on my siblings' faces when I really tried to be a part of things, a part of conversations, a part of the madness my family considered fun at our gatherings. Too often my thoughts and my expressions were simply ignored, or I was told I didn't know what I was talking about. The more I was ignored, the greater the wedge was between us.

In my mind, I lived my life in a home where I was an invisible man. This invisibility was also a factor in creating suicidal thoughts. This also made me feel worthless, cheap, like a piece of petrified feces. There is no psychiatrist, clinical psychologist, clinical counselor, or psych medication that can make petrified feces alive again. I see now God was setting me up to understand life is a matter of spirituality, and that was the only way my petrified state could be transformed to a living state.

FAMILY NEVER LETTING THINGS GO

I always felt like my siblings and Mom and Dad would just ask questions, questions, nagging questions about me.

They would ask me everything about everything that was going on with me, especially if it was something that bothered me. Overly inquisitive and overbearing to the nth degree. Nosy too, very nosy like I cannot even begin to get you to comprehend how nosy they were. Imagine you were with the nosiest people in the world all day long, and then finally you get to go home to sleep, and there's another nosy person sleeping in your bed waiting for you. That's how nosy.

Let me ask you something. If you were barely hanging on for dear life, if every moment of everyday you were just barely hanging on by a thread, every ounce of your energy was focused on survival, would you really want to hear all these stupid questions about your well-being? Questions about how you are doing? It's like rubbing salt into your already mortal wounds.

The most asinine part about this was that if you became upset with their nagging behavior, and snapped at them, they would regard you as the bad guy, deny anything truthful or rational that you said, and go on and on until they got to the bottom of whatever they perceived to be wrong with you. You were put under the microscope, and they kept on in a fashion comparable to a bulldog. The atmosphere would become toxic from that point on, especially if you hurt their feelings. At this juncture, there would be no need in my even hanging around, because there would've been a negative bug in the air. Their atmosphere would sour any chance of there being enjoyment between us. This was one of the very ugly reasons why I couldn't stand being around them.

FAMILY BLAMING COUSIN

One of the things about my Mom and siblings, even my Dad if you can believe it, was that they believed that I had been turned to the dark side by my Cousin. As I explained earlier in the book, I visited my Cousin and my Dad numerous times over the years when I was in high school. I vacationed with them. Every time I left, I always had this uneasy feeling from my Ohio family, always. It was like this feeling of control, of them not wanting me to be away, especially not with my Cousin and Dad.

At this time in the past, my Ohio family trusted them far less than they do now, and the crazy part is that my Dad and Mom have known my Cousin for nearly forty years now. This man has stood by them through thick and thicker. He had been a vast wealth of wisdom and knowledge for them, but did they really listen to him and take his advice at the time? Heck no. My Cousin, the man who I look up to and love as a father, was distrusted by my immediate family, like he was some threat to me. What the heck is that nonsense? Really? After everything that I had been through, there was no one better suited to help pull me through the muck and mire. My family obviously wasn't up to the challenge of helping me out of death. So why is it that the second I left their presence, I started to heal and get better? All it took was leaving the hellhole I grew up in, and the people I was surrounded by. Can anyone else see the answer here? I KNOW I CAN.

The way I see things, if my Mom ever trusted the man, then there should've been no questions or fears about her son going to stay with him. I mean, did the last forty years not happen? Or am I just stupid?

Sometimes when I made statements in my family's presence, they would tell me that that's my Cousin talking. Again, this harkens back to when I discussed the fact of being disrespected and treated like I'm invisible. Only this time they were just outright fighting against my identity. Dismissing my words and telling me they belong to my Cousin is the epitome of ignoring my identity. It's like why am I here? You obviously won't acknowledge what I think. Am I not a human being to you? How can you be so blatantly disrespectful? I'm your brother for goodness' sake. You didn't even treat each other this way. My siblings at least listened to each other, but never to me.

I guess part of it was that I was the baby of the family, not grown up like them. Not like they were that grown up anyway, or that much older than me; they didn't have extensive life experience. And I guess the other part was that they were just full of it. It shouldn't have mattered how much younger I was than them. Oft times kids are smarter than their older counterparts; they have good ideas. Listening is a wise thing to do. Some of us just don't do it well, that's all. Or we choose not to listen.

The mood somewhat changed about my later visits. The siblings didn't approve. They thought I was being infected by them, changed, and not in a way they liked. Over time I began to see the difference in the way they treated me. Obviously, they didn't like the fact that I was going to see my Cousin and Dad from time to time. Even after I lived with them permanently, it took my sisters four years to come and visit me when they realized I was not coming back to Ohio. It took my Mom five years.

As stated in a previous chapter, my Cousin was a Godsend. He was the first person to ever truly listen to me. The first person who ever really understood me and stood in my corner. He loved me unconditionally, a thing needed by everyone. He didn't judge me, didn't stifle my growth, but encouraged me, and helped me to heal. With him I was able to grow spiritually, emotionally, and mentally. I was able to start healing from the horrors of my past. And he helped me begin to discover and learn who I truly am. Without him I would be dead right now.

I thank God for putting him in my life because I was never going to receive any of this good treatment back where I grew up. I am still learning and growing with him to this day. We are constantly learning to the end of our lives.

HEARTBREAK

It has come to my attention that I need to divulge one of the most vital pieces of information that has lingered in my heart all these years.

And that is the very point right there, the heart. My heart was rent, ruined, and broken. And not just once. Because of my circumstances, the dishonesty of it all, the inability to speak my truth and be heard only prolonged my ordeal, causing fresh bleeding and breakage on a daily basis. It just didn't stop. The heartbreak was renewed again and again almost every time I dealt with my family. It became emotional, mental, and spiritual agony, to the point where I started to hate them. The hatred festered until I felt the desire to kill them.

It's a heartache that I feel to this day, and why it's taken so long for me to move on with my life. Now that should go to show you how deeply this affected me. If that's not proof enough of heartbreak, then I don't know what is.

The worst part about it is that after all this time, after all that I felt during the years of recovery and healing, they still have absolutely no idea how I feel right now. They have absolutely no idea of what turmoil I went through. To them it doesn't exist. This is an important lesson for those who suffer through something similar. That for some people, their truth is denied by those closest to them. There is an oblivious nature about their loved ones that precedes this. It could be anything that causes this oblivious nature, but in my case, it was simply that my family was living in a different reality than I was. Obviously, what I was going through was not a problem to them. It wasn't a problem because they did not see it as a problem, but just because they didn't see it as a problem doesn't mean that it was not.

They didn't believe that they were doing anything wrong. Their definition of family was nowhere near what mine was. In an unconditionally loving family, the suffering that I experienced would never have existed. In an unconditionally loving family, they would have at least acknowledged and accepted that my reality was different, my truth was different than theirs, and stopped attempting to force me out of my own and into theirs. Next, they would have at least tried to understand my reality, my truth, but they didn't. Instead, it was all resistance and intolerance. Like trying to make a wall understand my plight. Deaf ears, scrambled brains, nothing stuck. For me my family was the epitome of dysfunctionality. Coupled with that classic dysfunction, my family also had no spiritual relationship with God. Not only on the natural side, but the spiritual side. I was in a cast iron frying pan, just being burnt to a crisp.

Every time I would try to explain things to my Mom, it was literally like an input output table you learn about in mathematics. My Mom's brain was an input output table, only the equation that ran her table was all screwed up and wrong. My words would enter her mind, input, and then they would rearrange or become lost in a mess of her confused and convoluted mental reality, output. NOTHING GOT THROUGH. PERIOD. END OF STORY. So, more heartbreak. More disappointment. No support. Nothing.

It was at this point that any trust was long gone. Trust was dead. Heartbreak was alive, but I was dead inside. And I had completely stopped trying to explain things, gain support. I had ceased my arguing with my Mom. Every time my Mom would try to stir things up to make me change, I just took my Cousin's advice and went to my room, or put my headphones on and didn't listen. What more was there to say? What more was there to talk about? It was over. There was nothing left to bicker and banter on about. This at least taught me how to cut things off with people who won't listen. That it's better to just leave them be. Don't try to change them because what is the point? And if they try to confront you, just let them, and don't argue back. What can they do? They can't force you to argue with them. And when they know they aren't getting through anymore, when you ignore and/or don't listen, they either shut up or go crazier, at which point you need to get up and remove yourself from the environment where they are. If they try to follow you, as my Mom literally did, then you need to stay calm, do not use violence, and go to your room, or leave the house entirely until you both calm down.

My Cousin basically said, "If you don't want to deal with her nonsense anymore, then you need to learn to walk away and go to your room. Defuse the situation by doing so. Not only that, but simply don't respond. Don't argue back with people. It just does not do to fight."

It takes two fools to argue, and I am not a fool. It takes one person to break another's heart, and it takes continued ignorance to multiply that heartbreak by the thousands. This is how it felt to me. Heartbreak by the thousands.

RECLUSE

I was beginning to see that fighting with my Mom was pointless, trying to get her to see my truth was pointless. As I've mentioned before, she would not listen at all. She was convinced that she was right, bolstered by my clinical counselor, one of my siblings, her sisters, and friends, all of whom were always whispering in her ear. So really, I wasn't just fighting her, I was fighting all of them. It's a good thing I didn't own a gun because there would have been some bullets in people's heads. It wouldn't have mattered if they were my kin.

I would not give ground, period, I was not giving in to this crap. I can't tell you just how maddening it was that my Mom would not listen. It drove me absolutely insane and still boggles my brain to this day when I think about it.

So, I started to do what I had to do, which included cutting off from her. Ignoring the nonsense even when she was standing in the room talking at me. I put headphones on and listened to music when she was bombarding me. If it really got heated and insane, I would just go to my room and leave her be.

Sometimes, when she couldn't take that I was walking away, she would follow me through the house. That was a little scary because now she was starting to get physical. This one time, she was getting so crazy with her tirade that she was getting in my face. All I was doing was sitting at the table, listening to music on my headphones, reading a book on my tablet, all whilst eating some cereal, and she couldn't take the fact that I was ignoring her, that she wasn't getting through to me, that her reality was not being accepted by me. You have to understand that my Mom comes from a group of women, sisters, who are very domineering females, but that does not work with me, no matter what. Added to this was the fact that I had gotten to a point in my life where I was pissed to the highest level of the pissivity meter. My pissivity had overflowed from the scale and was causing a yellow tsunami to cascade over my surroundings.

My Mom was getting enraged at me more and more often too. It seemed like no matter what I was doing, she was throwing crap my way. I could be playing video games in the living room, minding my business, not even looking at her and she was getting angry and starting something with me. So as time went on, I began to retire more and more to my bedroom.

LEAVING HELL

I think it's important to emphasize to my readers that I needed to leave that place I grew up in. I needed to leave or else I was going to die there. I couldn't stay. I couldn't stand to stay in that place any longer. It's a place of death to me. The memories there are of such pain and suffering that even a simple family visit was painful for me. I don't want to go back. I cannot live there now. I will not, never again. My future children will grow up away from that place and live far happier lives than I did growing up.

One day, my Cousin called me up and told me that he and my Dad were coming to pick me up, to pack my bags because this time I was not coming back. So, I did just that.

I told my Mom who, like my siblings, was under the impression that this was just another temporary trip. Nah, she didn't like it, of course, and didn't waste any time making those last few days perhaps the most hellishly intense fights I'd ever had with her. What an ending, huh? Ending in flames.

She was at work when I left. At this time, my siblings all lived in their own places, my two sisters and my brother had graduated from college and were beginning their adult lives. I didn't leave any note or make any grand in-person goodbyes to her or my siblings. I didn't want to. Why the heck would I? After everything I'd been through with them. No, I wanted to slip away quietly, and that is exactly what I did. I didn't care what they thought of it, and just like that it was over. I left with my Cousin and Dad. I walked out of hell.

Can you believe that? I want you all to just think about that for a minute. After everything I just told you about my early life, I was able to just up and leave. Like none of it ever happened. Like none of this even existed to my family there. No one to stop me. None of them were there to bar my way. Because my truth didn't exist to them, because my clinical counselor had convinced them that I lived in the science fiction world and would not know reality if it bit me on the face.

Let me be clear. My truth did not exist to them. They had no idea that I was living in such peril and turmoil. And even if I had told them in its totality, which I attempted at least in part with my Mom for years, they not only wouldn't have listened, but they wouldn't have accepted it. You see, because in order for them to accept my truth, they would then have to admit that there was something wrong with themselves. And I can tell you, there is some seriously stubborn Irish and Slavic pride in my family. That stubborn pride is the downfall of many people; my family was no different.

And that is the sad part about it to me; it was like I was walking out of a psycho carnival. It demonstrates the sheer emptiness of it all. The fact that they were not there both physically and spiritually. That they were so unaware of my situation that they were not even there to say goodbye to me in the end. I'm not saying I wanted them there, what I'm talking about is the lack of their presence in my life, proven true in those last steps out of hell.

The farther the car got away from Ohio, the brighter the prospects of my future began to look. Mind you, it was a partly cloudy day, but for me, it was all sunshine.

GREATER LESSON

There are people in your life whom you trust to have your back and your heart. Ones whom you may fool yourself into believing have your best interests. But you are young and naïve and don't know any better because you are growing up, and you don't know yourself yet.

And even more heart rending, you don't really know the people around you. Your loved ones. Their hearts are more confused and tainted than you know. They don't have your best interests at heart because they don't really know and understand you, because they don't know and understand themselves. So how could they be in any competent position to help you.

They think they know better, but they don't. They act like they know better, but they don't. They end up thoroughly disappointing you, repeatedly, in a way that breaks your heart down to the very core of its essence. They destroy your life. This is no exaggeration. This is what happened to me.

I can state this with utter assurance about my family, my clinical counselor, my friends from school. They all disappointed me. All hurt me. All broke my heart.

I hated each and every one of them at various points of time throughout the years. I may not have known it at certain times, but the hatred was there.

The point is to learn to let go of your hatred. You cannot hold on to it. No matter how well founded it is, you must let it go, for you. It's nothing but poison in your veins. The only person it hurts is you. It may hurt the people you have directed it at, but I promise it will hurt you more.

Believe me. I understand what hatred is. I've been there and hated not just one person, but many, all at the same time, and not just my immediate family, but extended family too. Especially my extended family.

You must learn to forgive them all so that you can free yourself, and the only way to forgive a person is through God.

You may think you are forgiving them on your own, but you're not. There is no way you can forgive someone on your own. It's not in the nature of man to forgive. It's in the nature of God to forgive.

PART 2 - LIFE AND REBIRTH

LIFE AND REBIRTH - PART 1:
THE BLAME GAME

It took me a long time to wake up from this slumber of suffering, forgotten identity. I had to step out in faith many times, as we all need to. In fact, launching this book has been one of the greatest acts of faith in my life. It is mental and emotional release; it is setting me free; it is leading others to Jesus so that He can bring the change and set them free. That's a win-win in my book, no pun intended.

One thing that I didn't get until recent times was that, in my mind, I had built up this blame complex of hatred directed at my family. I blamed them for everything that happened to me, held them all responsible, when really, deep down, I actually hated myself.

This is a very big and important lesson that many people seem to miss. All your fiery emotions, thoughts, and actions which you've allowed to take aim at your family, friends, or acquaintances are actually just an external expression of your self-hatred.

Let's begin by saying that my parents were both very much this way when they first met and had not risen above their self judgement and issues of self-esteem, therefore it was bound to affect their children. So, I got a double shot of spiritual self judgement from day one of my life inside the womb. Repeat, if you grow up in such an environment, that spirit becomes a part of you if there is no one there to correct it or teach you otherwise.

For many years, I had started to judge myself, until it became so normal that it was like breathing. I didn't even know that I was doing it. It had become life. A diseased pool of self-judgement. Self-judgement is a very serious problem, especially amongst younger folks who are growing into who they're going to be for the rest of their lives. It's a very dangerous quality to have in this part of a person's life, because if left unchecked in their maturing stage of young adulthood, it can cement and become a strong part of their inner foundation.

If you're not careful, self-judgment can breed depression, and thus self-hatred. And when you hate yourself, your legs are in the cement, and it's very difficult to break free from that. Some folks never do break free. They become settled in their ways, into their self-hatred, using it like a comfort zone; a barrier or buffer to protect themselves. It's used like a shield and a sword. At that point, it has become your god, and that is not cool, my friends, because it will eventually take your life, or that of someone else's, or both.

Self-hatred becomes like a cloud around your mind. A cloud that distorts your reality of the world around you, skewing your view of yourself, and that of others. You are not seeing the situations in your life clearly. You start to live in your own sense of warped reality that is out of touch and tune with the real world.

You begin to hate everyone and believe that everyone hates you. As a result, you take everything they say, do, and think as a personal attack. You believe they're being nasty with you, treating you like you are some dog when really they're doing no such thing. You view

117

everyone as malicious individuals who have a personal vendetta against you.

You view your situations wrongly, thinking things are unfair, and completely stacked against you, when in fact they're often not. You even start to project your own inflamed thoughts into the minds of others, as if they think these terrible things about you. Thus, you've turned them into weapons to hurt you.

And lastly, many of the things you do, say, or think, seem to never be enough, never sufficient. You feel you are inadequate. Your words come out wrong, your thoughts seem to be muddled and unclear, and as a result, your actions have become an extension of this. Everything you do, say, and think, seems to fail.

You feel like you are in shambles, in total jeopardy, in flames. Your life is on fire, and your spirit is in a state of dying. You are malfunctioning, and you have no idea why it's happening, let alone how to fix it, and this goes on for years. Your suffering compounds until you see no other way out, but death.

This is an invisible menace that many people simply cannot see from the surface. It's like the coronavirus pandemic, which has affected so many people. Self-hatred is a silent killer, and many people seem not to care about this at all. And that hurts me. It makes me very angry because I have been through it. I know what that self-destructive force feels like.

That being said, it's time to talk about the solution, or cure for this. Just to give you an idea, the first twenty years of my life I went through all the madness previously stated in this book. Imagine sitting in it for that long, and then feeling the crushing impossible weight of the fact that you have to go to college and prepare for the rest of your life. I wasn't there. I was so far from even thinking about that point, the future. All that was on my mind was making the suffering stop and having a vacation. A very very very very VERY VERY VERY VERY VERY VERY VERY LONG VACATION. YEARS OF VACATION.

It was only when I moved away from all that crap, and lived with my Cousin, who showed me God, that I began the process, with God's help, to dig myself out of this mess. For the last eight years I have struggled, fought, cried, bled, until I reached the top of the mountain that God had led me up. Eight years of working this stuff out. That's how extensively damaged I was.

There was absolutely no way that I was moving forward with my life, going to school, starting a career, having a wife, raising a family, until I had at least moved beyond all this anguish. There would have been no functioning otherwise. I needed God to heal me first.

One of the greatest and hardest lessons that I had to learn was to forgive myself. I may not have had an ideal upbringing, but I was the one who allowed myself to fall. Not my family, nor my friends, nor my situation. I did it. My parents should have done better and done more, but that doesn't mean they're the ones responsible for my fall. I alone am responsible for my fall, because again, it was my choice to fall. I had to forgive myself, so that I could be free once and for all. This is how healing starts.

A large amount of people think of forgiveness mostly in an external form, not an internal form. They think of forgiveness in terms of forgiving others, or others forgiving them. People forget that we must also forgive ourselves for wrongdoing, and particularly for self-harm.

The first step in forgiving yourself is acknowledging that you allowed something wrong to happen to you. You made a conscious choice to allow that to happen. Forgiveness means admitting you did something wrong, and then releasing yourself from it, and how many people can you name off the top of your head who will admit that they're wrong? People don't like being wrong, much less facing the reality that they are, so they pin the wrong on others. This happens so much in life, especially now of days, that it's laughable. Grownups are not much different than children, really. You can picture two adults having a disagreement in the present day and liken it to two children playing with blocks. The children get mad at each other, one throws a tantrum and says, "I'm taking my blocks, and I'm going home!" And that is two adults today, in a nutshell.

When we pin the wrong on others, this is called the blame game. It's easy to blame others for bad things that happen to us, especially if they're the ones who hurt us, knowingly or not. We throw the problem at them and expect them to fix it, but even if they repent for what they did, they still can't fix what's broken inside us. Nor is it their responsibility. You see, it's harder for us to take responsibility for our own actions when we do wrong, but we have to take responsibility. Stop playing the blame game.

LIFE AND REBIRTH - PART 2

There is more than one way to lose your family. I spent the first twenty years of my life trying to fit in with my family. According to my perception, that alone indicates that there was already a problem, and not necessarily with me. Why should anyone ever feel the need to have to fit in or blend in with their own family? Now, I'm not crazy, and I'm obviously not stupid. If I felt in my heart that there was something wrong surrounding them, and it drove me to be something I'm not in order to fit in, then where does the problem lie?

It was fear that drove me to do this. The ongoing problem was this fear manifested itself doubly, fear of not being accepted, and fear of knowing others were placing me in a pool of uncertainty. It was pretty clear to me from what I felt in the atmosphere surrounding my family, and what I knew in my heart, that my identity would not have been agreeable to them, and at many times would have outright shocked them. My reasoning of life simply did not share common ground with theirs.

The truth of realizing that I did not fit in and could not fit in was too horrifying to accept or imagine. I believe I was in a state of denial. I spent all those years trying to fit in, only to realize that I did not; the truth is that it was impossible for me to be something and someone that I am not. Attempting to be something I wasn't, was very painful for me. It caused an eating away of my emotional stability, what little bit I had.

It was simple. They were crazy, their ways were crazy, their mannerisms were crazy, and I was nothing like that, but because I was outnumbered, I had to accommodate their craziness by betraying myself, betraying my nature. I did this because they had already demonstrated that they didn't understand my true self. They often thought I was totally crazy, lost in the sauce because of my personal interests, my opinions.

I endeavored to be more like them. This may seem totally asinine, but at the time it was the only right strategy for me to employ for my survival, blend in. The alternative would have been the ugliest form of all out nuclear war with my kin in which I would have used the truth to destroy them, and more than likely would have ended up killing them all. This last resort form of warfare happened anyway between myself and my Mom as I simply couldn't restrain myself anymore. I'd hit my limit with my family's madness. I would not do it anymore.

I think when I realized that I could not fit in, it hurt more than I can convey because basically that meant that I didn't really have them. I was not able to be with them as myself. I felt like I lost them, and that knowledge, that truth, was like I could be with them and not be with them. I could be among them, but never really felt like I was one of them. It just would not work. It was too hard to be myself amongst them because I would have stuck out like a fifth wheel.

I've told you all this so that I can make this point. You have got to be who you are in this world, no matter what. No matter how scary it may seem to do that, you have to if you want to be free. If you want to be free, then you must be *you*, the identity that you were born with, who God created you to be.

In order to do this, you have to *know yourself*. Know who you are. Don't think it, don't say it, but know it. Know it from your heart, not from your mind. Know it until it becomes like breathing. You also need to be at a place where you are not influenced by what other people think. What other people think, do, or say should not matter to you. It should not factor into your identity, or your perception of yourself. Everything that people say, do, or think regarding you is just noise, just loud noise in the background. IT DOES NOT MATTER. People will either hate you or love you. Leave it at that and live your life.

BE WHO YOU ARE, BE YOURSELF. You must. Life will be too heavy otherwise. If you choose to live as something you are not, you may be able to keep it up for a while, but I promise that eventually you will break down. You won't be able to do it anymore. It may even take you to your death, or close to it like it did me. To live this way is to live like a shadow of who you are. BE YOURSELF.

The lesson behind all this is fear. Fear is what drives us to live outside of ourselves and our identities. People have all sorts of fears, usually consisting of very specific things like spiders, or heights, or the dark. Others have fears of things that happened in their past. These fears stay with them and are often triggered by something that happens in their present. From my experience, fear of the past is considerably more binding and terrifying. This is because I allowed it to become a part of me, and as a result, it took on a reality in my present, infecting it with unhappiness.

My greatest fears are the past itself, madness itself, fear itself, and death itself.

I guess the fear of madness itself came into existence through a combination of things. One being that I was around family members who had very convoluted and overcomplicated ways of thinking, some of which bordered on insanity or outright insanity. I believe my Mom's and Dad's minds were tempered by the abnormal familial upbringings they received from their own hyper dysfunctional families. These neural patterns of thinking were never addressed nor confronted nor changed, they simply lingered on like rotting flesh, turning to gangrene and poisoning their lives.

They didn't even realize that this behavior had become normal, had become their very existence. And so much of this behavior was passed down to their children. My siblings seemed to follow a great deal in some of these ways, not all, but some. I always felt some form of resistance inside me to this alien nature of thinking and madness that seemed to permeate my family. As I grew up, I began to think of it all as a psycho circus, because there was nothing wrong with any of it, to them. Only wrong to me. They held to their truth, and I to mine, and there was no way in hell that I was going to give ground when I knew in my very heart that something was very wrong, and it was not to do with me.

I believe that over time as my mind became more and more fractured by the daily unintentional hurt and wounds inflicted by my family, particularly by my parents, I began to lose my mind. It's scary when you feel broken, and you don't know why, you don't understand. My family members are not savage or malicious people by any means.

Yet they sure didn't help matters any, and staying around them was only the equivalent of sitting in a cloud of poisonous death that was cutting me apart one sliver at a time. Pretty soon there would have been nothing left, and they would have been visiting me at a gravesite. They didn't know what they were doing to me, as I said, unintentional hurt; but they didn't know how to help me either, they could not.

The second part of all this was the results of my downward spiral. The clinical counselor, the psychiatrists, the psych medications. Be treated enough like a crazy person by different people, including your own family, and you will begin to believe that you are crazy. Especially when they send you to the psych ward, then you'll really get treated like a crazy person.

When you are in a place that is a dumpsite for mental patients, whose families don't care about them, or don't know how to care for them, then you will receive a great and powerful education as to the true definition of madness.

When you are around people who are truly mad, at varying stages or degrees of mental deterioration, and you yourself are not crazy, then you are exposed to all that and begin to spiral into it as well. You may develop a certain level of fear of it all, and not even realize that you are afraid of it. Not until later when you have started to heal, do you begin to realize that there may still be some residue, or fear of slipping back into madness. Many people deal with this issue, they just don't talk about it. It's an insidious form of evil that destroys you from within, but I declare and decree that I will never go back to it. That is my choice. You can also make this choice, readers.

Now, onto the subject of fear itself. I can tell you right now, that if your greatest fear is fear itself, then you are one step ahead. Fearing fear means that you are aware it must be combated.

But there is one thing that must be made absolutely clear to the masses of confused people. A lot of you, my readers, may believe fear is something that you can completely be without, never feel again, or something that you can step out of forever. This has been your hope and goal to achieve, and it's something that society and our misguided parents have taught us to strive for. This is not possible. It's delusional. You are looking at this completely wrong. You must transform the way you think regarding fear because you are always going to have some fear in this life, that is just being human. You will never be completely without fear, it's unrealistic to think otherwise. You will always have to keep it in check. There is no magic wand that is waved over your life, and it's suddenly gone forever, never to return. No, but if you are simply aware that it's a thing that must be combated, then you are already on your way.

Furthermore, my readers, you must STOP SEEING FEAR AS A NEGATIVE THING. FEAR IS A GOOD THING. Fear often signifies that you are ready. Ready for certain things to happen in your life. You are ready to take certain steps. Fear can signify that you are ready to step out in faith; the same way that I was afraid to step out in faith to write and publish this book. To reveal so much of myself and my heart to this world, I was not without fear. Fear was very much a part of it, yet I did not allow it to stop me. You've got to learn to block it out or tune it out, and do things anyway, even if you are afraid. Get comfortable being uncomfortable.

I was especially afraid of my family knowing who I truly am, which they've never known from the very beginning. I was afraid of what they would think of me and my truth, and how they would react. The thing that I had to come to terms with was that it does not matter. What they think does not matter. What they do or say about it does not matter. I am not writing this book for them. I am writing this book to advance God's Kingdom so that other people's lives may be saved from suicide and death, and that they receive healing. That's what's most important, and fear cannot and will not hold that back.

Fear must be confronted, or you will never demonstrate the finest parts of your quality and character. Confronting fear is a wonderful thing because it means acting on the best parts of you. It means finding your heart and releasing the goodness of it. Fear is of the mind, but you are not your mind. Your mind is a part of you, yes, but the real *you* is centered in your heart, because that is where God resides, in your heart, and He uses your heart as a conduit to speak to you and through you to others.

Operating from your heart means operating on a separate plain from your mind. Your mind makes so much noise, so many thoughts, because that's its job, that's what it's meant to do, and if you are not careful, then you will allow that noise to carry you away with it and change your fundamental nature. At that point, you can no longer hear your own heart anymore because you have stopped listening. You have allowed your mind to convince you that you are something else now. It has convinced you that YOU ARE YOUR MIND.

Your heart is a quiet place, a calm place without noise. It's clear, it's simple, and it's profound. That is what God is. His commands are simple, clear, and when He speaks, you will KNOW it's Him. So, if you have to wonder whether it's Him or not, then your mind is most likely making NOISE again.

Many people complain, "I can't hear God! Why won't He speak to me!? I've prayed and prayed!" Okay, how do you know He hasn't? In all likelihood He is speaking to you, and you've allowed your mind to make so much noise that it's no wonder you don't hear Him. And/or there is also a strong chance that you don't want to hear Him because He may have told you something that you don't want to listen to or accept, because in order to accept a truth that God says about you means that you must admit that there is something wrong about you. Something wrong that you are doing, thinking, or saying.

Numerous people seem to think that God will speak to them in that HUGE PROPHETIC VOICE THAT THUNDERS THROUGH THE SKY FOR ALL TO HEAR. "HEAR ME, MY SON. GO FORTH AND BLAH BLAH BLAH. YOU HAVE RECEIVED YOUR PROPHECY THIS DAY. BLAH BLAH BLAH. GOD BLESS YOU AND BLAH BLAH BLAH."

What you need to understand, my readers, is that while there may be times where God speaks to us in a way that is irrefutable, very strong and clear, God oftentimes speaks to us in whispers. I have had more experiences of God speaking to me quietly. Again whispers. You may have heard people say this before about whispers. It's true, and it points to a deeper truth that people don't want to accept. How God chooses to speak to you is up to Him, not you.

As you can see, fear of fear itself can spawn a slew of different things, all originating from your mind. And unfortunately, most people are ruled by their minds, ruled by fear. As I said before, people fear that they're not without fear. But always remember this. Without fear, there can be no courage. Without fear, there can be no bravery. Without fear, there can be no strength. Fear pushes us to rise, to become stronger, to overcome. So, if you really want to live in a delusion where fear doesn't exist, then you might as well erase the existence of courage, bravery, strength, and every other positive quality that's utilized to combat it. Then what are you?

Fear of death itself has been very real for me for some years now. I literally experienced it, the end, and God pulled me back from it. So yes, how could I not have a fear of death after that? That left a mark on my life. A mark that is being transformed into one of my greatest blessings, not only for me, but for others.

My fear has been of slipping back down that path to death once more. Death has a way of motivating a person. For those of you who have not had a real brush with death, let's just say that living becomes much more desirable after the experience.

Once you've given yourself to the Lord and He begins to transform you, then your greatest fear becomes a great source of strength, a great source of light and life.

And so, for me, fear had to come down, collapse. Fear of the past, fear of death, and the mental walls spawned by them. The walls that I had built up to survive, to protect myself from everything and everyone. Walls that I no longer needed. Walls that would take me no further in life. Walls and fortifications that had gone from protecting me, to becoming my prison. A prison that I carried with me wherever I went.

And for the longest time, I had such trouble breaking them down. Until I realized that it was impossible for me to do so. Only God could change my mind. So, I had to give it over to Him. Even then, I had trouble, because my perception was off.

I kept praying and praying and thinking that I had to move beyond the walls. When really, I needed to change my perception. I had to go from thinking of it as moving beyond, or breaking them down, and instead think of it as *there are no walls.*

I created the walls in my mind. So equally I could uncreate them. I could choose to see that they're no longer there. Let me reiterate that. It's not about breaking them down, or moving beyond them, because moving beyond them could simply mean you are moving out of their vicinity, but they're still nearby. No, you must choose to see that there are no walls. They no longer exist. By changing my perception to this, God was finally able to move and change my mind because I had gotten out of His way.

You created your mental walls, my readers. Now it's time for you realize that you can uncreate them, but you can only do this with God's help. There are no walls. There are no walls. There are no walls.

God is your protection. He is all the protection you will ever need. He loves you so much, and all He's waiting for is for you to depend on Him, rely on Him for your protection. He's waiting for you, not the other way around. So, what are you waiting for?

PRISON OF SHAME

A thing that had escaped my notice for many years was the subject of shame. I asked God, "What is this thing standing in my way? Why can I not enjoy myself around family? Why can I not take a compliment without embarrassment. What is this thing in my way?" And He faithfully directed me to the answer. Shame.

Over the course of many years of terrible suffering as I have described in this book, I had become so mired in shame. Shame was radiating off me as if I was a hazardous nuclear material. I was stuck in it to the point where it had become me. It had become everything about me, my way of life. It ruled me, and that is not an easy thing to admit. Remember, it took years of being away from where I grew up to realize what I had done and allowed.

Shame is often a self-inflicted wound. And the truth is that I allowed every single possible aspect of it upon myself. Not only that, but I lived with a mother who seemed to do nothing but shame me for what she believed to be wrongdoings, wrong behavior, or wrong ways of living, based solely upon the backdrop of her experience. If you grow up around someone like that, and a family which perceives you to be the one who must change, it can lead one to question himself or herself.

I was ashamed of everything about me. I was ashamed of my weaknesses. Ashamed that I was underperforming in school, seemingly unable to travel in the same direction of success as my classmates. When I took the SAT's at the end of my high school life, I knew that I had not done well. How could I have? I had just survived an extraordinary near-death experience after a childhood and adolescence based in human suffering. If you, my readers, had or have gone through such a thing, do you really believe that you could do well at anything? I remember that I got a ride home from friends, and we were all discussing how we did on the test. I remember lying to them, saying that I had done well, but had not finished a certain subject on the test. The truth was, I don't think I really finished any of them. I also remember seeing the disappointed look on my Mom's face when she saw my test results. I told her I didn't want to know the score, because at the time, it would have only salted my internal mortal wounds. And I know my Mom. There is no doubt in my mind she blabbed on about my bad test scores to my siblings, her sisters, and anyone she could possibly think of, absent my permission, of course.

My schooling was just one shame. Inside of the school I felt ashamed in my own skin. I was ashamed of my social standing, of feeling like I had no friends. Even to this day, they all seemed like shallow people. Not the kind of people you forge lifelong friendships with. I was not comfortable being around others. I was ashamed of allowing my friends to disrespect me and sometimes bully me.

I was ashamed of everything my family did, said, and thought regarding me. I was ashamed of how they treated me, how different their lifestyle was from what I thought to be good and right. I was ashamed of feeling like a disappointment that didn't measure up to them. At the time, I was ashamed to call them my family.

Each new day was a fresh open wound of trauma and pain. Every day was a new experience of agony, leading me one step closer to my deathly experiences down the road. Later, after I had left that place of death behind, I came to realize that I was ashamed that I had allowed myself to be so affected and influenced by my family that it almost killed me. I was ashamed that I had allowed myself to fall so far into hatred that I wanted to kill them. I was ashamed that I had allowed myself to fall into hatred, period.

I became so used to shame that it became passive. It became my armor, my walls, holding me back from life and light. It became the way I dealt with everything in life because it was all I had known for so long. It literally was my upbringing, my childhood, my adolescence. Shame was how I had developed, like some kind of corrupted cement pouring into my foundations as I grew. It hardened, and then it just was. It was me.

Shame was the prison itself, my thoughts were the bars, the cells. Prisons within a larger prison. I had created so many thought complexes. When your mind is warped or unhinged or in a depressed state, you can convince yourself that all manner of falsehoods are true, especially those that are about yourself. For example, you can convince yourself that you are ugly, when truthfully you are anything but. You can convince yourself that you are unintelligent or dumb. You can convince yourself that your family doesn't care about you, doesn't love you, when in reality they simply do not hold the same definition of love that you do. You can convince yourself that everyone hates you, when actually there are a great many people who admire you, but just don't know how to talk to you or approach you, perhaps out of shyness.

Shame walks hand in hand with self-judgment. Self-judgment opened the door for emptiness, neglect, and a deafening silence. While I lived among my family, classmates, and neighbors, to me I felt all alone. Though not all of it may have been intentional, I felt judged by everybody. This judgment is dangerous because my perception made it seem that everyone was against me, thus I complicated my life with the shame, the self-judgment, the anger, the anxiety, the complaining, and finally the judgment of others, bombarding me daily in many instances all at the same time. Why would these individuals neglect me? I had allowed my anger and emptiness to not only create a prison, but my own personal pit in which I saw no possible escape. I had created a contradicting dichotomy: a desire to escape by death while fighting a fear of death.

THE COLLAPSE OF NEGATIVITY

I had a dream once, that felt like a nightmare. I was standing in the house where I made the attempts on my own life. I was upstairs in the bedrooms. And in each room the ceiling had severe water damage; it was caving in, not quite breaking but close to it. I touched the area and felt the wetness on my fingers.

I was then downstairs, and I saw the same damage upon the ceiling, the same depressions, ready to burst and destroy all beneath.

I felt danger, great danger. I felt fear, not just of the situation, but an age-old fear of this place, and an overwhelming sense to GET OUT. I knew that even though the house was still standing, something terrible was about to happen. It was about to fall. So, I followed the sense, the instinct, my better judgment, and got to the back door.

My dog, Rory, was standing by the upstairs door, which led up to my room. I told her to come, and she half-heartedly did, but stopped part way. I told her to come again. She made another half effort, so I grabbed her collar and dragged her to the door. My dog ran outside. I was through the back door which led into a hall, turned to look back inside, and I knew the house was about to collapse. I could hear and feel it beginning to do just that.

Suddenly, an unseen force opened the adjoining slide door at the end of the hall and threw me backwards off my feet. I sailed through the open door and was finally outside the house. I yelled in fright and landed on my back. I watched as the house caved in, completely collapsed, and was swallowed up by a hole in the earth below. The ground sealed back together again, as if the house had never existed. I woke up yelling in a state of deep fear.

Now, it wasn't until I discussed this with my teacher, who is also my Cousin, that things became clear. For those of you who don't know and/or understand, dreams have a lot of symbolism, truths about what's happening in our lives. God speaks to us, especially in our dreams.

My Cousin helped me to realize that God was speaking to me heavily in this dream. Because of the negativity that I had built up throughout my years, my perception was off. I was seeing the dream all wrong. First, I was afraid, afraid of the house, afraid of the atmosphere in the house, afraid of the unseen force that had saved me.

God was showing me a great immeasurable truth of my life. The house that I had grown up in, the house where I had suffered and almost taken my life, was the source of all the negativity in my life. God was telling me that I had an attachment to this place, and it was an attachment that I could no longer hold on to.

The collapse of the house represents the complete and total end of negativity in my life. It represents God's work in destroying it and removing it from my being. It was also His way of assuring me that the negativity is being taken care of forever, hence the ground swallowing it, and all evidence of its existence erased.

The overwhelming urge to GET OUT, was a sign that my heart was in line with God, and because of that, I knew what needed to be done. That overwhelming feeling from God was His way of saying to me that if I continue to remain in the negativity of my life, it will eventually kill me. Literally kill me, somehow, some way. The house collapsing and crushing me is a symbolic representation of the negativity taking my life if I allow it, if I choose to stay in it.

God wanted me to know that I had formed a strong attachment to this childhood house. How could I not have formed a strong attachment to this place of death. A place where I had almost left this world. A place that had almost been my end. It only makes sense that this attachment had formed, because over the years after I had left, I had many dreams of being back in this house, and of being at the high school not far from it. A school where I was also being killed, little by little, every day.

My hopefully astute readers, many of you may not realize that when we almost die in a place, it leaves a spiritual mark on our lives. It's a place of significance to us, until God finally heals us, and we let it go. Then that place is no longer with us in its deathly form. We can't forget it, the place, but it no longer holds that significance over our lives. It's no longer our chain keeping us shackled. No, once we are freed from it, it adds to the pallet of our strength.

Read this part very carefully, my friends. Death in the framework of my mind became the worst possible end. It's definite, it's final. Which means that if you rise above suicide, then you have conquered that aspect of death. Let me say that again. IF YOU RISE ABOVE SUICIDE,

THEN YOU HAVE CONQUERED THAT ASPECT OF DEATH. When that happens, you have become immeasurably strong.

Not everyone is blessed and afforded such a gift of strength. If you simply change your perception, in other words, see with your heart, then you will see how this can propel you, and know that there is nothing you cannot do. Even now, years later, when I'm dealing with something particularly difficult for me to grow to or rise above in my life, I have to remind myself that I have conquered that aspect of death. I have been through worse than my current problems.

But I will tell you this, my dear readers, that if you take personal credit for your rising above death, and not give all the credit to your Creator, then you better get your mind right, because you didn't do it. There is no way whatsoever on earth that you can halt such an act as suicide and move beyond it without help from Above.

Go ahead, call me crazy. As far as I'm concerned, the only crazy people on this planet are people who live without acknowledgment or relationship with their Creator, who by their own choices make their lives infinitely and staggeringly more difficult. IF YOU REFUSE TO SAY IT, AND IT'S A CONSCIOUS CHOICE, THEN I WILL SAY IT FOR YOU. YOUR CREATOR SAVED YOUR LIFE NO MATTER HOW MUCH YOU BELIEVE OTHERWISE. MIRACLES LIKE THAT HAPPEN. I AM LIVING PROOF THAT MIRACLES STILL EXIST. HE LITERALLY SAVED MY LIFE. SAVED ME FROM MYSELF. SAVED ME FROM MY OWN HAND. AND NOW I AM AWAKE.

NOW IT'S TIME FOR YOU TO WAKE UP. SO, WAKE UP, PEOPLE.

CHOICE

Over the course of many years, my Cousin/Teacher told me over and over again thousands of times that everything in life boils down to A MATTER OF CHOICE.

Every single little thing that we do, say, and think is all a matter of CHOICE. Who we wish to be as people, our identities, IS A SIMPLE MATTER OF CHOICE. I CHOOSE TO BE HAPPY. I CHOOSE TO BE AT PEACE. I CHOOSE TO EXPERIENCE JOY WITH GOD.

Or if you want to act like an idiot, I CHOOSE TO BE NEGATIVE. I CHOOSE TO BE A VICTIM. I CHOOSE TO USE MY BAD EXPERIENCES AS A CRUTCH. I CHOOSE TO HOLD ON TO THE PAST. I CHOOSE TO HATE. I CHOOSE BLAH, BLAH-BLAH, BLAH-BLAH-BLAH, BLAH-BLAH.

This is the thing that many people tend to overthink. I am guilty of that same overthinking. For the first twenty years of my life, I lived among people who overthought everything. An entire community of people who would overthink. My parents were very much like this. And so that spirit was passed down to me through them, through their behavior. My siblings and I picked this up, and it became learned behavior.

This convoluted state of mind tore me away from my true identity. My heart. The identity that God birthed me to. Who God created me to be. Everyone has such an identity that God has birthed them to. Yet because of OUR CHOICES we become lost. Our environments, our parents, and events of our lives may screw us up, but ultimately, it's OUR CHOICES that determine which direction our lives take.

You can either CHOOSE to follow the path that God has laid out for you, or you can CHOOSE not to follow Him, and go your own way. But I tell you now, your own path only ends in emptiness and death. GOD IS THE WAY, THE TRUTH, AND THE LIFE.

Through God, you will experience that HIS WAY is the only way. The only reasonable way through life. The way that has the least resistance, the most comfort, and all the love, joy, and peace that you will ever need.

There are a whole lot of crazy misguided people in this world. One way that you will know them is when they say things like, "God is with us. We cannot lose. God is on our side." when their lives demonstrate they don't even know who God is.

Let's get this straight, shall we? GOD IS NOT ON YOUR SIDE IF YOU ARE DOING THE WILL OF YOUR father, THE DEVIL. THAT IS AN ABSOLUTE. IT'S THAT SIMPLE. IT'S ABOUT GOD'S WILL, NOT YOUR WILL. THE FACT THAT PEOPLE WOULD SAY HE IS ON OUR SIDE, SMACKS OF THE EGO, IDOLATRY, PLACING YOURSELF UPON GOD'S THRONE. GOD TELLS US HE IS JEALOUS AND WILL NOT SHARE HIS GLORY WITH ANYONE ELSE. SO, IT WILL NOT SUFFICE IF YOU CONTINUE DOWN THAT KIND OF PATH AND YOU WILL MOST CERTAINLY MEET YOUR END.

Okay. So, the point is that, over time, my mind became the center of my life. My heart was no longer the center. It may have been for a brief set of years as a child, but this all changed due to the environment I lived in and the people who were in that environment.

God is in your heart. Your heart is a direct line to The Father, The Son, and The Holy Spirit. Your heart is a piece of Him. By your OWN CHOICE, you may leave it in His care, in line with Him, or you can CHOOSE to make poor CHOICES, and over the course of your life your heart may become corrupt and evil. BUT IT'S YOUR CHOICE. IT'S BY THINE OWN HAND THAT YOUR CHOICES ARE MADE. GOD WILL NOT TAKE THAT FREEDOM FROM YOU. THAT IS FREE WILL. AND IF HE WERE TO CHANGE THAT, HE WOULD NO LONGER BE GOD.

My Cousin, Dad, and I traveled to Ohio for my parents' seventieth birthday party. It was a very nice and enjoyable time to be with family. This may sound strange given all that I have shared about my life and time spent with my kin.

But by this time, I had already begun to let go of many of my fears, angers, and insecurities with regards to them. Granted, it still felt nerve-wracking and turbulent for me just being around them and returning to the place of death that I had left far behind me, but as the week wore on, I found myself enjoying the vacation.

My Cousin was undergoing his final dialysis treatment for the week. I had been using the time to write at the treatment center. I brought my laptop, notebooks, and other writing materials into the lobby with me.

When it was getting close to time for my Cousin being done with treatment, I got my stuff ready, and took it out to the car. I had a multi-purpose laptop bag and walked outside at the same time as another patient did. We talked for a decent amount of time. He thought I was a stockbroker because of my bag and because I'm white. So, he made an assumption about me.

I told him I was an author. He was curious to know what I wrote. I spoke of a few different subjects and genres I've written extensively about, one of which he was very interested in. However, when I mentioned that I was writing a book about my suicide experiences, the conversation took a turn for the worse. The man had some kind of anti-suicide complex, as it seems a large number of Americans do.

In short words, the man basically told me that suicide doesn't matter, and that what I went through doesn't matter. That people who are suicidal are weak, and that everyone nowadays wants to kill themselves. He even suggested that I need to go smoke some weed to cope. Yes, weed.

My reaction was measured and calm. I didn't fight the guy on it because he was obviously a jaded person who was ruled by negativity, given the fact that he'd been on dialysis for two decades. He told me that he had two kidney transplants, meaning two surgeries that were successful, but eventually something went wrong with both, and he was back on dialysis.

There was no point in trying to get him to see the truth. I could have gotten pissed if I wanted to, but I didn't. Some people are just not worth getting mad about. I believe God meant for me to encounter this man to show just how ignorant some people are about the subject of suicide, and how necessary it was for me to write about it. I'll take things a step further. The patient was a black man.

Some of you, my black readers, may wonder why I would bring race into this. Simple, because it's indicative of how people from all walks of life, colors, backgrounds, can hold the same level of ignorance.

This isn't just a white thing. Although, I expect this level of stupidity from white folks, it demonstrates the widespread ignorance about suicide when you find black persons who act just as stupid as white folks.

One of the greatest lessons from this experience was this. You don't judge people based on what they've been through. You don't judge people, period. It's wrong. Flat out wrong. And it's even worse when you judge a person who is being open and honest about their past trials and struggles.

Who are you to tell me what constitutes enough or not enough to want to kill yourself? In this person's case, either he or someone very close to him attempted, and/or committed suicide, which basically jaded his outlook.

This is what happens when people trivialize the struggles of others, dismissing them as unimportant, when their knowledge, hides them in their secure box. Which is only secure to them; reality teaches us that they're most insecure.

And it speaks to a lesson that is far deeper and greater. One that so many, to this day, have still failed to learn. We, in this modern-day society of America, have forgotten one of the most powerful acts of human decency. Compassion.

Compassion – sympathetic pity or concern for the sufferings or misfortunes of others.

Where is the compassion these days? There used to be more of that the further back you travel in time. The older generations possessed more of this than the younger. The younger generations are almost entirely devoid of compassion. This is the age of me, me, me. What can I do for me? What can I do to elevate my position above that of others? How much attention can I garner on social media? How much money can I make for myself, alone?

With this kind of wrong thinking, there is no concept of compassion for others. It's like an alien word from another interplanetary dimension.

A stunning example that proves this was when I was helping my Cousin into a public building. I stood beside him, helping him walk to a bench to sit down. The room was chalk full of young people my age. Almost every one of them was staring at us like we were from another galaxy. I kid you not. It was like something out of a science fiction novel. You see, most young folks aren't thinking in a million years to avail themselves in service to an older person. They only think inwards. Me. Me. Me. There's an infinite number of other things they would be doing with their lives than coming to the aid of a senior. They don't even take care of their own parents. So, when they saw me with my Cousin, it was a sight that truly stupefied and puzzled them. This happens when there is a severe deficit of compassion.

The fact that human beings have lost this very simple yet fundamental part of who we're supposed to be, makes for a grim reality and a very dark future. A reality where people refuse to even look at each other as people.

We refuse to listen to each other's situations with compassion as that guy did to me, and instead view the world through a portal of dinginess. That dialysis patient was so twisted by his experiences that he would not acknowledge suicide as an important issue.

Hatred and selfishness are major causes for this kind of deadened and desensitized behavior. Again, that me, me, me complex.

So, it's your CHOICE. And you can CHOOSE right here, right now, to turn to God, and He will turn your life around. You can CHOOSE to make your heart the center, not your mind. And if that seems impossible, then ask Him for help so that you can hear your heart, feel from it, move from it.

The heart must be the CENTER. God must be the CENTER. Otherwise, your mind is ruling, and everything will be chaos. Chaos without form was what the world's condition was in before God spoke life and order into it. It's safe for us to conclude wherever chaos is, God is not; and wherever God is, chaos cannot abide.

This is the CHOICE that I had to make. It's different for everyone, so don't judge yourself on how long it takes to change, or how difficult it may be to go through the process. DO NOT COMPARE. DO NOT MEASURE.

It took me many years to grow and mature and heal from past hurts, from terrible horrors in my life. But as I have gone on and changed, I realized that I had to stop being hard on myself because it was no small thing what I went through. I lost my family and almost died because of it. They're still living, of course, but there is more than one way that a person can lose their family.

It was through the experience of suicide that I was able to truly come to God. Through it, He remade me, molded me, forged me, transformed me into what He designed me to be. He would use me as a means to heal others who have suffered the same.

I know that some you, my young readers, may have just been waiting for someone your age or close enough to it to speak up about it in a way that you can understand and sympathize with, because let's be honest, there are a great many adults who don't get it, or just don't care. That's alright, because that's their problem, not yours.

We got to talk about this stuff, young folks. But we have to talk about it in a way that hasn't been done before. We have to talk about this from a place of GOD. Because listen, all the scientific, medical, therapeutic crap does not do the job well enough. I know because I have been through it all, as I have explained in great detail earlier. I have been through the medications, the counselor therapy, through the hospital, and the group therapy.

So, I will give you one final example of how EVERYTHING IN LIFE IS A MATTER OF CHOICE.

The problem with most individuals who don't have a spiritual life, no relationship with God, is that they find means by which they 'think' they have hope. It's a facsimile of hope. It's something that is not lasting, it's something that is not firm, it's something that is not sturdy enough to carry them through the storms of life. And therefore, in the end, they realize that they didn't have hope at all, and are right back in that same chaotic, mixed up, disjointed, dismembered relationship that they were in before.

And for some, the suicidal thoughts come back. For some, the running away from home thoughts come back. For others, it manifests in a way where they start hating humanity. And that is the problem with false hope. Hope that is not centered on something that is lifelong. Spiritually, hope is eternal. Which means that the only way to have it is to have a relationship with God.

The teachers who run these scientifically and medically based group therapy sessions are living by the textbook. They're generating help by the textbook. They live there. That is what they promote. That is what they believe. The textbook becomes their God, it becomes their Bible. Everything fits into the textbook, and that's why spiritually minded people, or people who love God, can't go to just a regular counselor. They need to go to a counselor who is spiritually oriented, and God oriented, who's not just going to be a textbook geek, but they look at the textbook resolve, and then try it or challenge it by the Word of God. And that is what a Christian counselor is going to do.

Now you see, when I was in the young adult group therapy, medically recommended after my first suicide attempt, it felt like I was finally having some change, or breakthrough, because I was actually talking and connecting with people at a time when I had no friends. The friends who I had in school just didn't feel close. The folks at therapy felt like people I could finally share stuff with and talk to, and it felt like I had finally connected, for once. And that felt very good.

It wasn't until the group therapy reached its end, when I got away from all of them, that I realized, wow, it really amounted to nothing. And that can make a person feel absolutely horrible. For me, I remember when it ended. I drove out of there by myself. I didn't even go home immediately. I went into the park, at night, and pulled into one of those small parking lots on the side of the road. I was listening to crappy music that I liked at the time. The music wasn't having the effect on me it normally did, failing to comfort me. I just felt horrible. I had a loss again. There was a feeling that things were caving in once more.

It wasn't long after that when I was back in school. It just felt like everything was falling apart again. And after mere months of futile struggle, I went home and had my second suicide attempt. After months of adhering to a spiritless treatment in therapy, it had absolutely no effect on me, a spiritual person. The group session was over, but obviously that was not enough for me. So, why wasn't that seen by the professionals?

That is what I mean by people who live in the textbook. They can't look beyond the textbook. They don't have a real connection with their people, their students. That would take a spiritual relationship with God.

And here's the thing, I had missed a session during the months long journey, and how it worked was, once the whole therapy was over and I graduated, I had to go back and make up a session, but I was with a different group. That makes no sense, but alright.

Some of the people who were there towards the end of my original group run were there at my make up session, because as the original group therapy stretched over the months, more people flooded in and joined us. Some of the faces were still familiar, but a number of them had gone, the ones I had started out with. So, it felt scary and unfamiliar all over again. Not the brightest move on how their system was set up for fragile young people. Again also, this just made that lack of connection to the teachers glaringly apparent.

I said all that to say this. The therapy teachers CHOSE a textbook approach to all this young suffering, rather than an authentic spiritual approach, a Godly approach. Therefore, everyone that they were trying to reach and teach, and help rise above their problems remained lost even after the program ended.

Again, a simple CHOICE that could cost others so much once they realize that it did not help them at all, but instead left them with emptiness and a sense of crushing doom.

As you can see, the consequences of CHOICE can be a great blessing if you CHOOSE RIGHTLY. They can also be very costly if you CHOOSE WRONGLY.

Remember, my readers, that you have it in you to make the right CHOICE. Sometimes we may not always CHOOSE right. You're going to make mistakes in this life. Sometimes, the right CHOICES may not seem clear.

Remember that God created you. Saying that you don't have what you need, or that you can't do it, or that you are too weak, is like saying that God made a mistake, and God does not make mistakes. HE'S GOD. Everything you could possibly need is already inside you. God put it there. He is there. He is in you. He put what you need inside you. IT'S IN YOU. You have what you need to change your CHOICES, so that God may change your life forever.

You are never doing this alone. He will always be with you. He is guiding you. And if you just believe that He is already doing it, as in taking care of your situation, then you will see a change in your life the likes of which you've never known.

REMEMBER, I CHOOSE TO BE HAPPY. I CHOOSE TO BE AT PEACE. I CHOOSE TO EXPERIENCE JOY WITH GOD. SAY IT OUT LOUD. SPEAK IT INTO EXISTENCE. I DON'T CARE IF THAT SEEMS CRAZY. PEOPLE TALK TO THEMSELVES ALL THE TIME. DO IT. YOU ARE CHANGING YOUR CHOICE AND YOUR ATMOSPHERE BY DOING SO.

SPEAK IT AND YOU ARE CHOOSING TO SEE THE POSITIVE, RATHER THAN THE NEGATIVE. CHANGE YOUR PERCEPTIONS. CHANGE TO THE POSITIVE. FOCUS ON THE GOOD THINGS, NOT THE MESS.

The Bible says in Phil 4:8 "Finally, brothers and sisters, whatever is true, whatever is noble, whatever is right, whatever is pure, whatever is lovely, whatever is admirable - if anything is excellent or praiseworthy - think about such things."

Think on the good, my readers, and good will become you, good will become your life. All you have to do is make a simple CHOICE.

I simplified it to a phrase. If I think on the bad things, my life will be lost. If I think on the good things, my life will be found in God.

RISING ABOVE HATRED

Hatred is corrosive, destructive, and turns people into animals. Too many have succumbed to it in this world. That is a CHOICE, a willful CHOICE. No one is born with hatred. No one forces it upon them. It's learned behavior, CHOSEN, and accepted. Sometimes we grow up around hateful people. For example, racism is taught to children, but once they grow up, they're no longer children. Therefore, they now have a CHOICE to make. Continue to be hateful, despicable, ignorant, hypocritical, intolerant, bigoted human beings, or become learned, unconditionally loving, kind, fair-minded, and joyful persons. And the only way for that to happen is for you to have a relationship with God.

You don't change yourself; God does. Don't make the stupid selfish mistake that you are the one who changes your life, you don't. No one can have a true change of heart, but by God.

It almost always starts with something smaller such as fear or anger. These smaller emotions can fester and become hatred. Whether by external punishment due to other people's actions, and/or by your own self punishment. Often, it's both. When it's really bad like in my case, it's both.

Then your hatred fills up to the brim of your life, and spills over everything. Suffering begins because of hatred. That suffering tears holes through your spirit, your mind, your heart, and your soul. This destructive tempest compounds itself and grows ever more damaging as it spans over a period of years in your life. This is often the case for many if the issues are left unchecked and unresolved.

Poor parenting, poor household environments, things that happened in the past, abuse, molestation, anything can be the cause, really.

But what you, my young readers, truly need to understand is that this is not all the influence of others that caused you to go down this path of hell.

Take a deep breath and strap yourself into your chairs. Whatever your circumstances were or are, whatever happened to you because of events, or how others treated you, you allowed yourselves to fall into hatred. You made the conscious CHOICE to let it flood over your life, permeating everything you do, everything you say, everything you think, and everything you are.

Over time, you may grow to like it, not want to let it go. You feel as if it's well founded. You may even grow to a place where you wish retribution, revenge, especially upon those who are closest to you whom you hold responsible for your suffering.

As I explained in the first part of this book, I had grown to hate my family. I hated them with such a passion that I wanted to kill them and didn't even want to be around them. I didn't go to family events because I didn't have the energy or willpower to deal with them. When they came over to the house, I stayed in my room. I had had enough of them. They didn't realize they were unintentionally pushing me down a path to death, and I didn't have time for it.

They were not malicious people by any means, it was not their intention to hurt me, but hurt me they did. Whether it was their intention or not does not change the fact of how I felt back then, or in the years following.

One thing that I had to wake up to was that many of the hateful feelings I had about my siblings were not based on their actions but based on my perceptions of them. Stuff that I made up in my mind, thinking that they were terrible people, for example.

It's important to state once again, my readers, a thing that took me years to come to terms with and accept as truth. I MADE THE CONSCIOUS CHOICE TO ALLOW MYSELF TO FALL INTO A STATE OF HATRED. NO ONE MADE ME DO IT. MY FAMILY DID NOT. MY CIRCUMSTANCES DID NOT. I DID IT. ME. BY MY OWN HAND, DID I FALL. AND WHETHER YOU WANT TO COME TO TERMS WITH IT OR NOT, MANY OF YOU HAVE DONE THE SAME. YOU JUST DON'T WANT TO ADMIT IT. THE SAME WAY THAT I DID NOT WANT TO.

BUT ALL IT TAKES IS ANOTHER SIMPLE CONSCIOUS CHOICE TO DO THE RIGHT THING. SAY IT OUT LOUD WITH ME. SPEAK IT INTO EXISTENCE. I ALLOWED MYSELF TO FALL INTO HATRED. BY STATING THIS TRUTH, I AM ON MY WAY TO FREEDOM.

YOU HAVE TO TELL THE TRUTH TO YOURSELF, AS WELL AS TO OTHERS IN THIS LIFE. THE BIBLE SAYS THAT THE TRUTH WILL SET YOU FREE.

Perhaps the most profound knowledge that God imparted to me on this subject happened while I was praying and writing this very book. I was in a deep state of reflective prayer, looking humbly at myself, examining, seeing, admitting. I realized that I had never apologized to God about the hatred because I had been so wrapped up in it for so many years. So, I told Him that I was sorry about hating my family and myself. I told Him that I was sorry for wanting to kill my family, as well as myself.

Afterward I knew that God was pleased. I felt it. I heard Him say that He forgave me, and that He absolved me of the sins of hatred. There was a heartfelt sense of peace, relief, and uprightness. I felt like I had finally reached a place where God could move this poison from me. The valuable lesson He taught me next was that we can hate for so long that we forget how to love. Hate becomes all we know, until the love and innocence we retained as children is but a memory. I remember the wonderfully strong love I held for my family as a baby, and then as a young child. But I also recall how it began to fade and die off as I grew into adolescence and adulthood. So as a grand total, I knew hatred for more years in my life than I did love.

We as people in this country have allowed ourselves to become so accustomed to hatred. Americans are so full of hatred, spitefulness, and malice that we have become desensitized to violence in our communities. Let's be honest, this country has been bathed in atrocious sins since its conquering and colonizing, depending on which truthful term you wish to use. Notice I did not say founding because that is a friendly term. This country was not started on friendly terms. It began in violence and hatred,

157

and whatever begins in violence and hatred will continue in such a manner until a stop is put to it. Until people have a change of heart, and as I mentioned earlier in the book, the only way for people to have a true change of heart is to have a relationship with God.

Neighborly, brotherly, sisterly love has been replaced with a paranoid delusional reality that everyone is an enemy, and that we must protect ourselves, always have our guard up. As God taught me about myself, we need to learn to love again. We as fellow citizens, need to learn to love one another again the way that God intended.

MY LIBERATING EXPERIENCE

Coming from a small town, my interaction with blacks was limited. My high school was 85% white, 4% black, 9% others. The school marching band of 160 or so members, only 5 or so were black, and finally my neighborhood, none were black.

While my interaction with blacks was limited, whenever my Cousin would come to Ohio and I would have my weekly visit with my Dad, I was drawn to him and didn't know why. As I grew older, I started to realize there was more to this than face value recognition. While communicating with my Cousin, who is a black man and my blood relative, I learned so much about my McKnight family that my parents didn't tell me because the dysfunctionality of their families was the only reality to speak of.

As you remember reading in previous chapters how my teen years catapulted me into a chaotic abyss, it was my calling him on the phone that helped me maintain a semblance of normalcy. I had the opportunity to go to Delaware two different years for Christmas vacation. I was so happy to arrive, but sadness and depression overcame me when it was time to leave. In my heart I wished I could stay and never return to Ohio, but I was still a minor and the custodial child of my Mom.

It was only after the relationship with my Mom tanked did she threaten me with shipment off to Delaware. This pushed me even further away from her because to me it appeared that she was throwing me out into the streets.

At the time, it didn't occur to me that permanently moving to Delaware was a possibility, so that was the farthest thing from my mind. My Cousin tried his best to console me so that I would not go over the edge. He promised me better days were coming. With all the telephone communication and many vacations, I was getting to know my Cousin even better. He is a pastor, a college professor, a husband, a father, and a brother. As he shared critical parts of his life story with me, my eyes were opened to the fact that my family was dysfunctional.

During my childhood experience, my point of reference from both my paternal side and maternal side amounted to zero. Once a year, I saw my paternal grandparents in Myrtle Beach, SC for one week. Every other year my maternal family would meet in either the Outer Banks, NC or Kelleys Island, OH.

My Cousin's family on the other hand, got together for Sunday dinners after church, had picnics and vacations together during the year, were always communicating with each other, and basically had an overall loving relationship with each other. I wasn't prepared for that nor was I used to that. It was getting close to the time for me to graduate from high school and my Mom's sole concern was for me to enroll in a local community college. As I shared with you, I was in no position within or without my being to go to college. I honestly believed my Mom would have recognized that truth. The overall problem was she would not accept it because she was more concerned about the alimony payments being cut off.

This only made conflict heighten in our home. But I had one ray of hope. As I've stated previously, my Cousin informed me that he and my Dad would be coming to Ohio to pick me up, and then we would drive to the Outer Banks, NC for vacation. That was the best news I could have received. Even though the relationship with my Mom escalated to a back and forth shouting match, in the back of my mind I could see the Outer Banks.

As the time drew close, my Cousin let me know that he and my Dad would arrive on a Saturday, and that I needed to be ready. On that Friday, it was almost like I heard angels singing because my Cousin called and said, "Ryan, pack all of your bags and everything you want to bring with you. You will not be returning to Ohio. I love you and I'll see you on Saturday."

It felt like a flood of light and relief and hope blossomed within me. I don't just mean this in an emotional way, but in a profoundly spiritual sense. It was like for once I had a breath of fresh air, but the air did not come from outside. It was as if the air had spontaneously materialized inside my spiritual lungs, and I felt a breath of life after so much deathly struggle. And now the deathly struggle with my family would finally end. Seemingly, Saturday couldn't get here quick enough.

The first thing I remember feeling when my Cousin and Dad pulled up into the driveway was a sense of heightened elation and joy. For once a genuine positive feeling, something good happening in my life. My Cousin came through the door first and hugged me, and it was a rather long and emotional hug. My Dad stood happily behind him waiting before he got his hug. My little cousin DJ, my Cousin's grandson, was there, overjoyed to see me. I made sure I gave him a hug.

We got the stuff packed into the car quickly, and we were out of there before I knew it. I had told them beforehand that I didn't want to say goodbye to my family. I wanted to slip away quietly because emotionally and mentally that was easier than having to deal with my family's drama. I literally didn't have it in me to go through a goodbye. I was too drained.

The duality of my Mom's drama would have been overwhelmingly trying. While she would have been acting like she didn't want me to go, in her eyes you would see her relief that I was leaving. I chose not to see my siblings because they didn't trust our Dad nor our Cousin. I took one last look at the house, gave my dog a hug, and out we went. Rory had this thing where she would stand on her hind legs, with her front paws on the windowsill and watch us drive away.

It was a beautiful sunny day, which made our trip even nicer. We drove halfway to Hagerstown, MD, where my Cousin had secured a room for the four of us. We picked up dinner and went back to the motel.

I was enjoying my interaction with my cousin DJ, for he was quite the comical little fellow. We talked about Nintendo 3DS games, PS3 games, and much to my surprise, life. I found it very interesting how developed his worldview was at eight years old. We got a good night's rest, and we woke up to enjoy the motel's breakfast. The remainder of our trip to Delaware was pleasant, we went right to my Cousin's and Dad's apartment. We unloaded the car, had dinner, slept well, and in the morning, we dropped DJ off to a friend's home, and we were off to NC.

This began the more serious interaction with my Cousin, which was informative, transformative, and life building. But it was not easy for him, because I had built so many walls of protection that it was difficult for him to get beyond them. The more I trusted him, the easier it was for the walls to break down. One of the other factors that aided me in getting even more close to my Cousin was the fact he needed a Caregiver. And I believed that my purpose for being in Delaware was to take care of him.

One wall that needed breaking was the withdrawal I was experiencing as a result of stopping the psych medications. It appeared to me that this was going to be a long journey to my overall freedom.

I began tackling one of the greatest hurdles of my life. Discovering who I am, learning I do have worth, and becoming confident in who I am. It was not easy and my Cousin had to demonstrate a saintly patience. I would not accept I had any worth because of the negativity I grew up in and the lack of family values projected by my immediate family and my paternal and maternal dysfunctional families.

During this time of learning, I came to realize through my Cousin encouraging me that my family did not hate me, but actually loved me. To my readers, pain and depression can be so strong that vision is clouded, and the person creates mental scenario upon mental scenario to justify their feelings. Prior to me coming to Delaware, my psychiatrist kept me drugged up. My clinical counselor tried filling my head with psychoanalytical textbook feces. I am so glad my Cousin showed me that God loves me, protects me and comforts me; I just didn't know it at the time. I will discuss the spiritual evolution of my life in the next chapter.

It's important for my readers to understand, particularly parents, who have depressed and possibly suicidal children that it takes a person who has a real relationship with God to aid in bringing that child back. As I discussed with you in a previous chapter, I have learned through my Cousin's teaching that life is a matter of CHOICE. The righter CHOICES I made, the lighter my life's load was. Interacting with my newly met family caused me to see new and brighter horizons in my life. I have come to the conclusion that there is a distinct difference between black families and white families. I know I'm white, realize I can never be black, but what God has allowed me to witness and learn from my blood related black family is priceless and I would never exchange it for anything. So, as I conclude this chapter, please note that the man I witnessed as a child and came to later learn was my Cousin, God also made him the Father figure in my life. This in no way is meant to diminish or demean my biological Father's relationship or position in my life.

BREAKING OF THE MIND -
TRUST AND FAITH

I remember that during the Homegoing Service of a dear Cousin and family member, the Lord spoke to me. I heard the words, *You're about to break.*

I knew in that moment that He meant it as a good breaking. Being at the Homegoing Service was very difficult for me, but the reason it was difficult was because I was holding on to things that I had no business holding on to. I was carrying too much weight in my spirit.

The main reason that I was suffering so much at the Homegoing Service and the following events was simply because I was holding onto anger. Anger that was so deep-seated that it became passive, so normal that it was like breathing. It was in the very fabric of my blood, my veins and arteries; it had become me, and yet was not me, not me at all. It had nothing to do with the true character of my heart.

Nevertheless, it was in me, in my spirit, and had to leave. The time had come for the spirit of anger to die. It was a weight, a stone that had to be left on the ground. Stones do not belong in humans; they belong on the ground.

You can be angry for so long that when asked what you are angry about, you don't have an answer. You don't even know why you're angry anymore. Whatever screwed you up as a child, you have dwelled in for so long that you can't even answer a simple question. What are you angry about? Can you actually think of a solid reason right now? Something real and legitimate?

I had become this way, and it clung to me like a residue, a dead weight dragging behind me in everything I did, so much so that it robbed me of love, joy, and peace. Because of it, I had not fully accepted God's Grace. It had become so routine that when it was time for it to go, it was a great shock to me to begin the process of letting it go. Obedience, trust, and faith did not come easily to me in that time. I acted so stubborn and with such fuming anger, that I was in danger of delaying God's blessings.

Thankfully, I mustered the wisdom of my heart to start letting go. And the only way that was possible was because I acted on my trust and faith in God, that He knew what He was doing, and that this was His battle, not mine.

That is so important. His battle, not mine. You are not meant to fight these things and fix these things yourself. You must surrender them to Him. Surrender your mind to Him. I had to reach a place where I realized and accepted, "God, I'm tired. I can't fight these things in my mind anymore. I don't have the strength. I can't control my mind. I can't control every little thing I worry about." Then I began to put it in His hands, and let Him take care of it, as He is meant to.

Let it be clear, even if you could control your mind, even if you had the power to move the mental problems out of your way, you were never supposed to in the first place. If you are, then you have taken God's place. You might as well kick Jesus off His throne and sit there yourself, because you sure aren't leaving Him in charge. You're trying in vain to take charge of your mind, your life, and run it how you wish, and how you think it should go.

Have fun because you're not going to get anywhere with that.

There were other days where God was showing me that the extreme self-judgment and doubt had to end. These traits and all negativity resembling them had no place where He was taking me. This was rough to accept, but it became plain to me, like with the anger, that I was going to have to commit all these negative habits to God, and stand in TRUST AND FAITH.

We as people become so focused in the wrong direction, on the wrong side of the spectrum of our issues. All our attention is honed on the objects that hurt us. Pain, anger, fear, doubt, disbelief, self-judgment, trauma, the past, whatever it may be. We push against it with all our might, hoping to dislodge it, but nothing we do seems to make it go away. So, we sit with it helplessly like guard dogs standing watch. We sit like slaves next to our problems. And oft times, there are so many of them happening simultaneously.

There is a better way, dear readers, but that better way involves TRUST AND FAITH. You must learn to seek God first above and beyond everything else going on in your life. When you do that, everything you're dealing with, everything that could possibly concern you in reality and in your mind, will be taken care of.

TRUST AND FAITH are paramount. They should be more important than anything else to you. They're something that you must keep renewing. Even when you are at the place where your TRUST AND FAITH is in

God, and you know He is taking care of your lifelong issues, you must still keep your TRUST AND FAITH in Him daily, no matter how hard it gets.

One day, I had to pause and take a moment to breathe, meditate, and ask myself what was most important to me? What did I desire most? What did I want out of this life more than anything? The answer came to me before long, and it was simple.

I want peace. I want peace with God, and the peace of God, after a life at war.

FAKE IDENTITY - ANGER

I've been angry my whole life. If you're angry your whole life, it becomes all you know and the only way you know how to behave. It forges into a habit, and that habit becomes you.

That's why breaking the habit is very hard to do, even if you have forgiven the person, persons, or things responsible for your anguish, the habit continues to persist, independent of your will.

On the tail end of this anger, there grew a great perspective. A perspective that grew more and more every day. When my Cousin was speaking to me, the reason I didn't want to make eye contact with him was because I was so angry inside. Repressed deep anger. So normalized, so much a part of my cells, my DNA, that I didn't even know it was there.

It became a part of everything I thought, said, and did. I spewed negativity like exhaling air, transforming and poisoning the atmosphere around me. It responded to everything positive. Every time there was a positive, my mind's automatic response was to find a negative, or begin with negativity before positivity, always.

The same way I didn't want to make eye contact with my Cousin, I also didn't want to make eye contact with people in general. These were the walls I held up between myself and others. The anger was the fuel that upheld the walls in my mind. Without the anger, the walls would fall down.

So, you see, when you are angry, you erect barriers and cut yourself off from everyone around you. Then, with those walls, you are blinded to what's outside. You are so focused on the bad, you cannot see the good anymore. The good of life, in life, about life.

The walls have to come down. It's the only way to be free. What blocks you, hinders you, must be cleared. But not by the means that you may think. Not by bludgeoning yourself against a hard wall, but by targeting the anger. Whatever is feeding, fueling the anger, is where your wisdom must grow.

Again, not by means you understand. You need to reorient your mind into a new way of thinking. You are not the one who fixes this. You are not the one who does this, ending the anger. That's God's job. He does it. Not you. You need to learn to live in faith. Only have Faith and Trust that it's being done.

He'll take the anger. He'll take the fuel that holds your walls up, your prison upheld, until it all collapses into dust and nothingness.

Then He'll clear away the dust cloud with His love, and you'll see. You'll see the sun shining once again. As if for the first time in your life. You'll be glad you didn't give up. You'll know more than ever that life is worth living. You'll be glad you didn't kill yourself so long ago, because now you see the miracle. You see that you are a living breathing, walking, talking miracle.

You can see. You can see now. It's as if your eyes have been opened for the first time in your life. You can see life the way it was always meant to be seen. Through God's eyes.

Everything is different now. Everything is clear. Vivid. Lucid. Powerful. You can see. So, thank Him for that. Thank God for that. Thank God that you can see, and that you are now beyond suicide.

IDENTITY - PART 1: BELIEVE

When you arrive at the place of suicide, you have forgotten your God given identity.

People use terms like The Essential Self, The Universal Self. This country has become so steeped and mired in the works of people who don't know what they're talking about. They constantly reach outside the realm of God to their own designs and schemes to better not only themselves, but they pass on their hollow enlightenment to the masses like an infection, leading too many astray.

Look, life is not that complicated. The only way you heal is to accept that God is real. That there is something greater that is protecting us, no matter how cruel life is. Call me yet another psycho who believes in religion, even though I'm not talking about religion, I'm talking about God; there is a big difference. I realize there are those who will oppose me, and you're entitled to your opinion. Please remember opinions are on the same plain as anuses, and everybody has one; depending on the person's hygiene, some are cleaner than others, some just simply stink, and some are mired with the residue of fecal matter.

But guess what, folks? That's what faith is. You believe even though you can't see it. You believe God loves you and is protecting you, even if it doesn't feel like it sometimes. The more atheistic thinkers out there who are consumed by the need to prove that God does not exist and will argue against His existence till the end of their lives, will like always, persecute those who believe.

Again, guess what? I don't have to prove that God exists. That is not my job. And that is not how this works. An indisputable reality exists, I cannot prove God exists, and you cannot prove that He doesn't. It wouldn't matter if you gave them irrefutable proof that He lives. They would still deny it. It's happened before.

YOU EITHER BELIEVE THAT GOD EXISTS OR YOU DON'T. THERE IS NO MIDDLE GROUND. YOU EITHER HAVE TRUST AND FAITH IN GOD OR YOU DON'T. IT MUST BE ABSOLUTE. YOU EITHER BELIEVE ALL THE WAY OR DISBELIEVE ALL THE WAY. IT'S A CHOICE, AND A VERY SIMPLE ONE AT THAT. IT'S ONLY WHEN YOU ALLOW YOUR MINDS TO GET IN THE WAY THAT IT BECOMES COMPLICATED.

IDENTITY - PART 2: ACCEPT WHO YOU ARE

I put so much time and effort into this negative fake protective identity that I forgot who I was. When you spend so much time around negative people in a negative environment, and everything around you is negative all the time for your whole life, you start to become that way. You start to become negative, and then it becomes the only thing you understand.

At that point, positivity is just a foreign word, you don't even understand it. Then, no matter what the situation is, you always have to find something to be negative about. It becomes a habit, very strong habits develop in negativity, and then you're just walking around like a nuclear reactor in meltdown, and nobody wants to be around you.

I've shown you throughout this work just the number of things I was going through, and how that was the downward spiral that I experienced over a very long period of time. That journey in and of itself could turn anyone into a negative person. Once you've arrived at that negative nexus, you've betrayed who you are. You're a product of the environment you grew up in.

Between dealing with my parent's negativity, and my siblings' negativity, who my parents passed it down to, and also into myself, mix all that with the negativity of school, which was multiplied by hundreds of students, as well as every other crazy person I encountered in town, and you will have the sum total of local negativity I endured. When our school combined with a neighboring school, it became almost two-thousand students in a building that was not meant to handle that capacity. Couple that with the negativity of friends, negative encounters I had with people daily, public humiliation on a daily basis, going to see shrinks, a clinical counselor, and all the negative crap they offloaded into me, and it's a miracle that I didn't go psychotic and postal, and just kill everybody.

In addition, there was the business of going out every day into the public, whether it was the store, or out for a walk somewhere in town, public events. It got to the point where I didn't have the confidence, self-esteem, fortitude, and strength to even do that anymore. I stayed in the house like a recluse. I couldn't go out anymore. I couldn't even go into the grocery store anymore. I didn't have the emotional, mental, and spiritual stability to go shopping with Mom. She would do the shopping, and I would stay at home. If anything, I would wait out in the car while she ran the errands.

I was living in a literal cesspool of negativity. Day in, day out, every day, seven days a week, three-hundred-sixty-five days a year, for twenty years. Twenty years I sat in that negativity like a sponge.

So, I never had a chance for positivity to develop in my life; not even when I was a child. Positivity was a word I didn't know or understand. There was the positivity in my heart. I had that. That, God gave me. And that stayed alive, but dormant.

What I'm trying to say is that the positivity inside me, my true identity, was always there. It just didn't have a chance to come out, to truly live. Living as this negative self, I forgot who I really was. I didn't accept who I was anymore. I had accepted this negative fake self, this new self that was not me.

By the example of my life, I'm trying to show people the power of negativity, the power it has over your life if you allow it, especially if it's in your life long enough for you to know nothing else. You can't help the circumstances you grow up in; you're a product of your environment. That's what this is about. I was a product of my environment. I was around a whole lot of negativity. Too much. Far too much. It's a miracle I survived that. I survived things that would kill other people. And I am just now learning what it means to let the positivity have its day; for it to live and grow, to be in the light so that it can be nourished, and as a result, allow the real me to come back. I'm learning to stop the negativity.

All I do is follow God's path. Although, I can't begin to tell you how tired it's made me. This negativity has taken a toll on me, on my life. It's forced me to grow like nobody's business. I've said to people before that I feel like I'm two-hundred years old, but that inner age has afforded me a strength that I think few people my age have. I feel old, very old, yet in a young body, but that's okay.

We are who we are, even if we sometimes forget. You must accept who you are no matter what. You have to. Otherwise, you're already dead. You're living death every day. If you don't accept who you are, you are dying. You are in a de facto state of dying and death.

You want to live? Accept who you are, as I am learning to. This is so that you can live your life. Stop fighting, stop struggling. Live. Be who you are. You can't care what other people think, or what you think of yourself. You must move on from these things. Accept who you are, no matter what. No matter how hard it is, with all your strength, you have to. Accept who you are.

Don't fight it, don't resist it. Just let God transform you. He will if you let Him. Just accept who you are.

FAMILY

One of the greatest lessons in life is knowing that you have a family that understands you, truly understands you. This is so important, and that's putting it mildly. If you are in a family that doesn't understand you, inevitably there is going to be some heart rending. As if a piece of your soul and heart is missing. You feel incomplete without a strong understanding family.

For me personally, I received the family that I needed later in life, not the beginning. It was in this new family, my Cousins, that I began to find peace and acceptance in myself the longer I was around them. It's a gift and a blessing to have a sane saved family in insane times. And that's exactly the word I needed associated with my new family. Sanity. Anything less than that and I wouldn't have been able to handle them. I had been through an extraordinary upbringing, and therefore needed an extraordinary family, and that's exactly what God gifted to me.

God is Omniscient. He knew that I would need this kind of rare and special family. One tailor-made for me. He knew the heartbreak and fire that I would go through long before I was born. He knew then. He knew me. He knew that I could be trusted with such a family. He knew that I would need this family to find my self-worth, to stop wallowing in self-pity and darkness so that I would learn to bask in the light. Let God light up the darkness.

PROTECTION OF THE WOLF

Dreams can symbolize many things in our lives. Sometimes they mean something, sometimes they mean nothing and are just dreams. Some are not worth remembering, and others you will remember because they're important. They will stay with you, often until you gain clarification. It's not always easy, particularly when you are young and inexperienced, to know if they mean something verses no meaning.

I will share with you a dream I had years ago, not long after I arrived in Delaware. A dream I did not understand at the time, but that I knew was profound and still stays with me today. One that is very relevant for you to hear, young readers.

In the dream, there was a castle with dark ancient stone walls, a powerful fortress. The walls, the castle itself, I believe represented God. It represented how I was with Him, within Him, inside his Grace and Protection, and empowered by Him to do incredible good.

There was a great wolf roaming within the walls, fully grown, strong; a being that had been seasoned and weathered through much hardship, suffering, and toil. That being was me. The wolf was me. It represented me.

Surrounding the wolf were many, perhaps hundreds of little animals in their infantile states. All different kinds, wolves and many others. Although, the interesting thing about all these little animals was this.

There were no parents around to protect these creatures, no other adult animals of any kind or sort. The only adult animal around to offer any protection whatsoever was the wolf. Me. They were all so very helpless, mewling little things. Vulnerable to attack from predators.

The feeling in the dream was crystal clear. I was their shepherd, their protector. Who else was going to do it? There was no one else. And unfortunately, there was another literal problem on the horizon. First off, the entrance to the castle was open. Literally, there was no hinged gate to bar outsiders from entry. Only a tall, wide, empty, arched doorway in the wall.

On the horizon, was a vast pack of wild animals, predators, killer beasts. Wolves, wild dogs, wildcats of all kinds. Ravenous teeth baring monsters. All adult animals. Hundreds or perhaps thousands of them. I think you can imagine that these animals were not there to help. They were not the lost parents coming to reclaim their offspring. They were there to kill the little ones.

In that instant, I, the wolf, unleashed a deafening roar. It split the air. It sounded like a cross between that of a roaring lion, and a snarling wolf. But behind it all, was the sound of an unknown roaring animal, one that could not be classified, but strong beyond all measure.

At the sound of my roar, the ravenous beasts were filled with fear and fled back into the wilds whence they came, never to return. The little ones went on living, and I, the wolf, continued my purpose as their shepherd.

This dream represents or symbolizes a few things. The fact that the little ones had no parents simply symbolizes that I had no one there to protect me. You may feel similar to the way I felt, readers.

God made me stronger than most so that I would survive the tremendous suffering that I would experience later in life. I was tempered and became even stronger. You may ask, why would God do that? So that I would be strong enough to help you, young readers. I'm here, ready to help.

This is why, in this dream, God symbolized me to be the wolf, the shepherd. The protector of the little animals. Your protector, young readers. He wanted me to tell you that you are the little animals; that you have been through tremendous suffering, like me. God is ready to forge you into something greater. But it will take time. Your minds have been warped by your experiences.

One of the main points of this book, young readers, is for you to know the importance of the fact that your hearts are not the problem here. Your minds are the problem. They have been twisted, strung out, damaged, wounded, and warped. But no matter how much your minds devolved you did not survive because of them. You survived because your hearts are strong. Your hearts are why you are alive, not your minds. You are alive because God deemed it to be. He's not done with you.

It will take time for your minds to heal. All the hell you've been through will not go away with a snap of the fingers, and by the wave of a magic wand. It takes time to heal. I know this. I've been healing for years, and I'm just now coming out of it. Do you know how long that felt like? How it felt like I would never surmount the insurmountable brokenness of my mind? Of my emotional and spiritual woundings? How shredded up my heart was by the traumatic experiences? I'm telling you, it felt like I would never get beyond it. But again, that was my mind talking, and I couldn't and wouldn't listen to it. I had to learn to listen to my heart, trust my heart, trust God. Walk in Faith and Trust.

To trust your heart is to trust who you really are, your true identity. Who God made you to be. And to trust who God made you to be IS TO TRUST GOD.

God will send you the person that will help to free your mind, to heal your mind and heart. Like he did for me.

EPILOGUE: RISE

Now that I have taken you through my journey of fire and death and laid my heart bare, it's up to you to decide what to do with the contents and pieces I have shown you. It's up to you to make a CHOICE. What will you do? Will you choose to slink back into the hole that you have struggled so hard to claw your way out of? Will you choose to say enough, and finally begin working your way out? Will you rise?

Remember that the God of hope and peace is always waiting for you. He is waiting for you to reach your hand up so that He can take it and raise you out of your suffering. You will not have a pain-free life. This world hurts. It hurts very badly. But know that there is a God who is greater. Greater than all the suffering you have ever been through. Greater than pain. Greater than hate and rage. Greater than death. Greater than suicide. All you have to do is believe. Believe in the One who can stop you from dying. Believe in the One who can provide a way out of your situation. Believe in the One who can cause you to rise out of suicide.

Take it from my heart, take it from what I know to be true. YOU CAN RISE above suicide. YOU CAN RISE above depression. YOU CAN RISE above doubt and disbelief. YOU CAN RISE above defeat. YOU CAN RISE above despair. YOU CAN RISE into your healing. YOU CAN RISE into the person that God wants you to be. YOU CAN RISE into all the love, joy, and peace that God has to offer you. YOU CAN RISE into Faith and Trust.

This isn't some madman psychobabble that I'm spouting off here. I'm not a fanatic. I can promise you that when you turn to God, YOU WON'T BE THE SAME. My life has been restored. You don't know how much I have healed since I got to know Him. Whether you want to believe it or not, God is with all of us. He's always been there. His Hand was always on me through my hell. He was pushing me forward even when I was wandering aimlessly. He was there when no one else was. And I never would have made it without Him. Never. He pushed me through all that hell because I had a destiny to fulfill. And that destiny is fulfilled. It's staring you in the face right now in the form of the book you are holding. He pushed me through it all so that I could speak to you. It wasn't my time to die. I had to go on so that someone else's life would be saved, changed, healed, whatever they needed. Whatever you needed, dear readers.

I came out golden from the flames, and you will too. Just believe. Just believe. Don't ever give up, no matter what. And if you feel like giving up, reach out to God. Listen out for Him. You'll hear Him calling you to RISE! RISE! RISE!

Made in the USA
Columbia, SC
27 May 2024

35931691R00114